The Star Chernobyl

THE STAR CHERNOBYL

Julia Voznesenskaya

Translated from the Russian by
Alan Myers

QUARTET BOOKS
LONDON

First published in English by Quartet Books Limited 1987
. A member of the Namara Group
27/29 Goodge Street, London W1P 1FD

Translation copyright © 1987 by Quartet Books
Originally written in Russian as Zvezda Chernobyl
Copyright © by Julia Voznesenskaya
First published in German by Roitman Verlag, Munich, in 1986

British Library Cataloguing in Publication Data

Voznesenskaya, Julia
The star Chernobyl.
I. Title II. Zvezda Chernobyl. *English*
891.73'44 [F] PG3489.4.Z59

ISBN 0-7043-2631-0

Typeset by Reprotype Limited, Peterborough, Cambs
Printed and bound in Great Britain at
The Camelot Press plc, Southampton

The Star Chernobyl

CHERNOBYL (Russ) Large variety of wormwood.
Artemisia vulgaris
VI. Dal' Defining Dictionary VOL IV

And the third angel sounded, and there fell a great star
from heaven, burning as it were a lamp, and it fell upon
the third part of the rivers, and upon the fountains of
waters;
    And the name of the star is called Wormwood:
and the third part of the waters became wormwood;
and many men died of the waters, because they were
made bitter.

Revelation of St John the Divine
8:10-11

PROLOGUE

Once upon a time there lived three little sisters...

The sisters had been talking for more than four hours, sometimes sadly quiet, sometimes arguing heatedly. Three coffee-pots had boiled and been emptied, countless 'Capital' and 'White Sea' cigarettes smoked and still no firm decisions had been arrived at.

Anna got up from the sofa, walked about the room for a while, then approached the window.

'Midnight. The sky's getting lighter again...'

'White nights ... One dawn hastens to relieve another, granting night a bare half-hour,' Anastasia pronounced distinctly.

Anna winced slightly: she disliked her elder sister's declamatory tone, also her fondness for hackneyed schoolgirl quotations from Pushkin. She left the window.

'More coffee?'

'Well, why not ... We won't sleep tonight anyway, and I've been a long time without coffee.'

'Why on earth didn't you write? I'd have sent you some.'

'Oh, coffee's a luxury. I'm not going to start bothering about that or bother you either.'

'Coffee's not a luxury, it's a medium of communication,' Anna smiled. 'You're not hungry by any chance?'

'Who in the world eats at one in the morning?'

'Some do ... Well, I'll go and put the coffee on, and then we'll decide.'

As Anna left the room, Anastasia sighed, picked up a fresh papirosa, twisted the tube man-fashion and lit up.

She had journeyed to Leningrad rigorously prepared for this final talk with Anna, the last of their lives; she intended to lay before her sister everything she had been repressing for years, things she had forbidden herself even to think about. She was going to settle accounts with her once and for all.

She examined the room. What a lovely room it was! Give Anna her due: whatever the vagaries of fashion, she'd kept almost all their parents' furniture.

Mother's glass book-case. 'Dear, respected book-case!' She had explained the irony of Chekhov's words to her pupils. On her occasional visits to Leningrad, however, she uttered the words to herself without any irony at all whenever she entered her parents' old room. During the blockade Mam hadn't burnt a single book, she'd preserved all the family literary treasures.

The oval table too, solid oak, still occupied the same position in the middle of the room. Not that it could be moved to speak of – it might fall to bits. The chandelier above it was the same: antique, bronze, darkened with age. Come to that, things like these were back in fashion, according to Anna.

Once upon a time a happy family had lived in this room: husband, wife and three daughters, Anastasia, Anna and little Alenka, all starting with A. Five of them lived in these twenty-five metres, but Lord they'd been marvellous times.

Father had been a test-pilot, often away for long stretches at a time. Was that the reason he and Mother were so much in love? When Father was killed on Novaya Zemlya, Alenka was only three and Anna still at school; Anastasia herself had just finished teacher training and was intending to go on to a further qualification. She was regarded as gifted and an academic career beckoned. She had a young man as well, Volodya ... The whole lot came tumbling down in a matter of months. Mother never recovered after Father's death, she grew stooped and aged, her life extinguished in no time at all. Anastasia was left with the two youngest on her hands; boyfriend, further degree, all of it slipped away from her. The main thing to be decided was how to bring up her sisters. Anastasia volunteered to teach in the country, a remote village in Leningrad Province, it being easier there to provide for the little girls on a teacher's pittance. She used to let this room and it had proved a considerable help in their modest existence. When Anna finished school, she couldn't get into college straight away: village schooling was not sufficient to enable her to take the entrance exams. For a whole year Anastasia wouldn't let her go out to work; instead she put her through a course of intensive study herself. The following year Anna passed her exams with flying colours and started at the Herzen Institute; this meant no more tenants in their parents' flat since Anna would be living there. She did get two girl students to move in with her at a tenner each, but what was that, even added to her twenty-rouble-a-month grant? ... Anastasia did a spot of moonlighting and during the holidays got a job as a leader in a pioneer camp near Leningrad: that meant she could take Alenka there and have Anna close at hand. So life had gone on, and her youth with it...

Anna started kicking over the traces as soon as she graduated. She gave up her further degree course, then got married and immediately left her husband, got mixed up with dissidents, started signing petitions and spent a year in the camps for her pains. Of course she was no help at all, but Anastasia didn't expect any; she was just sorry that Anna had left the straight and narrow.

When little Alenka left school at fifteen, Anastasia was loath to send her to Anna; still it had to be done, she herself simply didn't know enough to prepare Alenka for college and where could she get in after a village school? Only a vocational place. Finally she made up her mind and brought Alenka to Anna so the girl could go to school in Leningrad till she was seventeen. Little Alenka was a cheerful, good-hearted girl, not interested much in anything, fond of nature and the countryside. Anastasia was sure Anna wouldn't be able to lead her astray among the dissidents and in any case Anna had sworn on their mother's memory that she would do no such thing. Her elder sisters had planned for her to train as a teacher and join the school where Anastasia had been headmistress for six years now, the same village school she had come to as a

3

helpless young girl with two little sisters on her hands.

And so, the week before, she had received Anna's letter saying that she had been invited to West Germany and that the authorities were not disposed to stand in her way. Anastasia was to come to Leningrad as a matter of urgency to decide Alenka's future. The letter arrived naturally at the most inconvenient moment, during the school-leaving exams. Anastasia had had to take, for the first time in fifteen years, three days' sick leave. She didn't have to lie about it, her heart had been acting up for a long time. So she had come to Leningrad to thrash the matter out.

On the way, she had prepared herself for the discussion, having a shrewd idea of how it would go. Anna would be off to her precious West Germany, but Alenka had her college exams coming up and needed supervision. Anastasia had weighed the matter carefully but, after some heart-ache, had resolved that really she had no choice, none at all: she would have to give up the school and her position there so hardly won, along with her cosy little school flat and move to Leningrad to take Anna's place. She was now entirely prepared for this, intending only, perhaps, for the first time in her life, to reproach Anna with selfishness and disregard for her sister's future. Those well-merited words were already composed: 'I brought you and Alenka up, and had no life of my own, just my work to keep me going. And now you're going away and destroying the only thing I have left – my chances of professional promotion; you're dirtying my good name – me, a party member. I have to give up everything I've worked for with my brain and my hands – the headship, the flat, my colleagues, and move into your share-kitchen place. I'll have to get some job in town where they've got so many teachers they have to work as charwomen practically. Do you know how much trouble you've caused me? Do you know how many times I've been interviewed by the KGB and questioned about you? It's a miracle I've stayed in the party. A miracle, you hear! You weren't afraid of the camps, that's your affair, but you didn't consider that I might be thrown out of the party and lose my job, did you? And now again you're doing just what suits your fancy, leaving Alenka in the lurch and going

4

away to your precious Europe. Of course I won't abandon Alenka but you might perhaps thank me for being a mother to you and giving up my whole life for you as well!'

It was wounding, even cruel, but deserved, she was certain of that as she reached the city. But suddenly it turned out that no carefully rehearsed reproaches were needed. The matter, it appeared, was far graver and more complex: Anna had no intention of leaving Alenka, she had decided to take her sister abroad with her. For this the elder sister was unprepared. Discussion about Alenka and her future had gone on between them for nigh on seven hours.

Anastasia finished her 'White Sea' and shook the packet – empty.

'No more papirosi, Nastenka?' Anna enquired, bringing in the coffee. 'I've got some stronger somewhere. Shall I get them?'

Anastasia realized at once that Anna had calmed down a bit watching the coffee out in the kitchen and had mellowed towards her. Well, she would wait and see how things shaped...

'Yes please, if you can find me something a bit stronger, I can't really get on with the grass you smoke.'

Anna smiled.

'That's what they call marijuana, Nastenka. Don't make me out to be a junky, God forbid the KGB gets to hear of it.'

Anastasia made no response to this, it was a feeble witticism. Anna's relationship with the KGB was no concern of hers, as she had said during all her interviews.

Anna found a packet of 'Aurora' on a book-shelf and placed it in front of her sister; she poured the coffee, seated herself and lit a cigarette.

'Nastenka! I know the efforts you put into bringing up Alenka and me after Mam died. I know you had no life of your own on account of us, I know that.'

'It had to be done, God, you know!'

'Nastenka, we did live in the country ... when I was growing up, the old wives told me everything. Because of you, they said, you tiny tots, your sis lost her young man, she wouldn't saddle him with two kids, it didn't matter

5

what he said. I also happen to know they tried to talk you into putting Alenka in a children's home and me in a boarding-school, but you wouldn't have it.'

'It was a really good boarding-school incidentally – all the teaching was in English. It would have come in handy for you now.' Anastasia sneered, touched by Anna's unexpected words and anxious to keep the feeling at bay.

'Well in Germany I expect I'll get by with my German. But it's not me we're talking about. Think of it like this, it's about time I did something important for Alenka, it's my turn now, don't you think?'

'No I don't. You took her on in town to finish her schooling, so thank you for that. Village schools can't get them up to college entry, more's the pity.'

'Yes, but that's only two years. And Alenka's easy to get on with – and she worked hard; you were mostly responsible for that as well.'

'Yes, I gave her extra-curricular tuition. Not just in history and literature either, by the way.'

'There you are then. Now it's my turn to start worrying about her. The girl will get a real education over there, see the world, learn languages.'

'Where's she going to study then, not Oxford by any chance?'

'No, well, what about Heidelberg, they've invited me to lecture there.'

'Anna, what are you blathering about? You have to pay to study there, where's the money coming from?'

'I can work for it.'

'What about all the unemployment?'

Anna crashed her cup down but recovered herself at once.

'Nastenka! Please believe me, real life in the West is totally, just totally different from what the papers say here.'

'Yes, yes, I know your dissident arguments. You don't even believe the papers when they say there's been an earthquake in Tashkent, everything's lies to you now.'

'My dear sweet sister, even when they print the truth, they can't help lying about something. Don't you remember that house collapsing on Mayakovsky? You know how

6

many people were taken away in the ambulance – and what did the papers say? "No casualties, thanks to timely measures." You remember, you were here for your holidays when it happened.'

'You can't take one isolated incident and make a whole system out of it.'

'That's not it, Nastenka darling, the system operates so that every isolated incident is prepared, packaged and presented in the way the system wants it to be remembered – in people's minds and in history as well. You're a language specialist and a historian, surely you must be disgusted sometimes when Russian history is turned into some kind of raree-show, just a series of well-displayed exhibits? Doesn't it ever turn you off, Stalin's role in the Revolution, Brezhnev's in the war? Go on, tell me, do you really believe in the history you teach?'

'Anna! You started believing in God, you got yourself christened. Do you understand everything in the Bible?'

'That's an odd question. Why do you ask?'

'No, no, you've got to answer. Do you understand everything in the Bible, in the text of the prayers? Do you understand every little bit of what your dissident priests say, with your mind I mean, or do you accept some of it as a matter of faith?'

'There's a lot I take on trust, but what's all this to do with the system?'

'That's your regime, your system, your structure. With me it's my faith in the party. There was a lot I had my doubts about, and plenty I didn't understand, but I do know the main thing – I believe in my party. It's blind faith, if you like, blind repetition of what the party teaches, but I believe that at the heart of our party, there are people wiser than you and I. If they do something that looks incomprehensible at first sight or even second, I have to have faith!'

'In anything they say?'

'Yes, anything. You go on reciting your prayers on trust don't you? Well for me every word of my party is as holy as that. That's what I put over to my pupils and because I believe, my pupils believe me. How could I teach them if I

7

had doubts myself, eh? You tell me. I *believe*, that's all there is to it.'

'So you see yourself as some sort of deacon in a church?'

'Yes, if you like. It's as good a comparison as any. You've got the same hierarchy in your church, the same discipline, the same blind faith, or trust rather. Trust in those entrusted with leading the people, being a shepherd to them.'

'Shepherd? You communists really imagine you're the people's shepherds?'

'Why do you think that's an insult? You've got pastors, so have we. You've got one faith, we've got another.'

'Hmm ... You know, Nastenka, there's some truth in that. That kind of truth's even more frightening than any free-thinking rebels have ever thought up. Isn't that what lies at the root of your militant atheism?'

'Perhaps it is, perhaps it is. You dream of spreading Christianity to all mankind. You've often told me yourself, how one of you came straight out with it in court: "We need the whole world!"'

'Volodya Poresh...'

'I don't remember your leaders' names, I'm sorry!'

'You reckon they won't go down in history so you needn't know their names?'

'No, indeed they won't. Their circle was narrow and far, far off from the people.'

'That's as may be, but Lenin wasn't prophesying about us. Still you do believe at least that these people, we that is, are acting out of conscience and conviction?'

'What difference does that make?'

'Well if only because your party tells lies about us. They've even invented a crime – "slander directed against the Soviet state and social structure" – now that's what I call surrealism. Jailing people for daring to tell the truth.'

'Their version of the truth, you mean!'

'Is that wrong?'

'It is if it harms the people.'

'Just why is it you party members are the ones who

8

decide what's useful and what's harmful?'

'Why? Because we *are* the people. Our circle's wide and we live among the people. Who do you think my villages would rather believe, you or me, if we had a mind to have this discussion in front of them?'

'Today it would be you, because they know you, they believe you.'

'Well, there you are, the circle's complete, they believe me. And they believe me because I believe in the party.'

'Yes indeed, you've driven me into a corner. I've only one objection to raise.'

'Go on then, try.'

'If we ever did set up a discussion forum like that would we both be arrested on the same charge?'

'Yes, because discussions like that are not allowed, but that's no argument.'

'Stop there, Nastenka. Where, and by whom were discussions like that forbidden – and when?'

'Everything that isn't done here or doesn't happen, shouldn't happen, that's why it's not allowed. Why don't they have discussions with atheists in your church? Or hold dances?'

'Yes I know, Nastya, you're a real tough, party battle-axe now. You'll be among the top brass yet.'

'Not now I won't.'

'Because of Alenka and me?'

'"Alenka and me" again? I've told you a dozen times, I'm not letting her go with you."

'What if she wants to?'

'She doesn't, surely?'

'She can't make up her own mind. Doesn't want to leave you on your own. She's sorry for you.'

'Thanks for not hiding that from me. It would be a pity if I had to keep her here against her will.'

'Against her will? You wouldn't go that far?'

'Oh yes I would. I'm responsible to Mother for Alenka.'

'Thank God it's not to the party.'

'To the party as well, but you wouldn't understand that. I promised Mam I'd see you were both all right. I got you on your feet and it's not my fault if you wandered off the right road. Now it's my duty – to bring up Alenka as a proper person.'

'No, but you wouldn't stop her if she wanted to go?'

'Yes, yes I would. I'm still her legal guardian.'

'In two months' time she'll have turned eighteen; she'll be able to make her own decision about her future. I can wait till the fifteenth of August.'

'Excellent. Let's just wait then. Till then let the little girl take her exams in peace. She's set on teacher training?'

'She's not set on anything, you know her. I told her "apply", so she did. But she's not doing anything about it, featherbrain.'

'Well, you know where she gets that from. All right, let's have a truce: you postpone your leaving, Alenka does her exams then decides herself – go with you or stay with me.'

'All right then, I agree to wait.'

'Till then let me take her off to the country for a couple of weeks, let the little girl relax before the exams. What's the time by the way? Just what I thought – after two! And where on earth is she wandering to at this time of night?'

'Probably seeing somebody else off. Since the leaving party it hasn't stopped, one boy going into the army, one girl off to college in Moscow ... and it looks as if she's in love.'

'Who is he?'

'I've no idea. You should know Alenka, she usually has plenty to say but she can sometimes keep things to herself and you just can't worm it out of her.'

'Well, there you are, how can I let a child go off with you, eh? I can imagine the bohemian life-style you'll have in Germany – or some place like Paris, God forbid.'

'For heaven's sake, Nastenka! Paris isn't some place, it's the one and only on this planet. Anyway what's wrong with falling in love at seventeen? Just the time for it.'

'Time for those with a dad and mam they're afraid of upsetting. Alenka's an orphan. Can't you understand that at least?'

10

'What sort of an orphan is she if she's got you and me? Here's us six hours on end dividing her up like a divorcing couple. Don't give me that little orphan stuff.'

'Oh, Anka, you and your emancipation! You know nothing about real life, do you? Suppose he's a no-gooder, a lot older than her?'

'If he's older does that mean he's a no-gooder?'

'Usually.'

'Know that from experience, do you?'

'You can't annoy me that way. Yes it is from experience if you must know, but not mine. A quarter of the little girls in our village are teenage mothers. How did it happen? It's the student working parties that come out in the summer. You get schoolgirls having babies in the fields. The interesting thing is, it's not so much the students, it's the leaders. So there you are.'

'Student working parties by the way, that's a party thing, so you can put the single-parent families on your account, your immaculate party religion. Or is it in the party's interest for schoolgirls to increase the birth-rate?'

'Anna, leave out the speechifying, I'm serious: where can Alenka be wandering after two in the morning?'

'Nastenka, darling, it's the White Nights! Didn't you go out when you were young?'

'Yes, but not for long. While our mother was alive. After that I used to wash Alenka's underthings and darn your stockings at nights.'

'So you're reproaching me with darning stockings! Oh, really, Nastya, you're high-principled all right, a heroine if you like, but you're hard.'

'Yes, I am hard. Hard, like a tank and dull as a mausoleum. Impenetrable as a concrete blockhouse. I've heard all that from you before. But I'm not interested in your opinion of my character now. It doesn't matter any more, seeing as we're parting for ever and, I hope, shan't remember one another again.'

'But why? I'll never forget you, Nastenka. I'll write, send parcels.'

'That's all I need! I don't want CIA handouts, thank you.'

11

'Get a hold of yourself, Nastya! What have the CIA got to do with it?'

'Where did the parcels come from when you were in the camp?'

'From our friends in the West.'

'Oh, yes of course, friends. Who needs you there? Who would be interested in the opponents of a regime in a foreign country?'

'But you work a day's overtime every year for the peace fund. That money of yours goes to the opponents of foreign regimes.'

'That money's not distributed by "friends". It's done by the appropriate organizations.'

'The KGB you mean?'

'Whoever's job it is does it. There as well as here.'

'Yes, that's logic all right. Except that yours is Soviet logic.'

'How could it be anything else? That's why I'm warning you in advance – no letters, no parcels to Alenka or me.'

'Why "Alenka or me"? We haven't decided about Alenka yet.'

'Who's deciding about Alenka then?' A voice rang out. 'You've been what, deciding my fate all night, while all good people are out on the streets?'

In the doorway stood their younger sister. Her dress was wet as if just washed; her fair hair hung down in rats' tails from which water dripped on to the floor. In her arms she held an armful of lilac as wet as herself. She looked at her sisters with mad, merry eyes.

'Alenka! Where did you get so wet?'

'In the Neva.'

'Lord! Did you fall in?'

'Na-a, I was swimming.'

'In your dress?'

'Why, d'you think I should take a bathing costume when I'm going to meet a boy? I didn't know I'd feel like a swim, now did I?'

'And where did you get the lilac?'

'From Pushkin.'

'You're not making sense. Did you take it from a

garden? You deserve to be caught by the police!'

'No, honestly, it really is from Pushkin! Today's the sixth of June, you know, Pushkin's birthday. So Ivan and I nipped into the garden of the Pushkin house on the Moika. You should see the lilac there.'

'You stole the lilac from Alexander Sergeyevich himself, then?' asked Anastasia; she was having difficulty repressing a smile.

'Nastenka, you know he won't mind! He'd be only too pleased if a boy took a bunch of lilac from his garden for his fiancée.'

'Don't talk rubbish, half-wit fiancée.' Anna spoke really sternly now as she started gathering up the dishes. 'Go and get changed or you'll catch your death. I'm making breakfast in a minute, but first have some of this hot coffee, it'll warm you up.'

'I'm not cold at all. Haven't you got anything else? Champagne maybe, vodka at least?'

'The belt's what you need, never mind champagne,' said Anastasia. 'Get changed and sit up to the table. We've got some serious talking to do, your future's at stake.'

'No decisions necessary. I've decided it myself already. Or rather Ivanushka and I have together.'

'And just what have you decided with your precious Ivanushka?'

'My future, I'm telling you!'

'How could you possibly decide?'

'Like the best sort of fairy-tale. Once upon a time there lived three little sisters. The eldest was clever, the middle one was beautiful but the youngest, Alenushka was – a fool. Their mother died, the elder sisters worked hard to bring her up but she grew no cleverer. And then they started thinking and wondering how they could get rid of the little fool, and get her settled. And then the physicist Ivanushka came to propose to her, a fool as well of course. Alenushka thought and thought ... three whole hours she thought! Well then she went and consented to marry him. They lived for a long time and died on the same day. There, that's the end of my fairy-tale.'

'Anna! Leave that washing-up, come here and listen to

13

what this wet little idiot's telling me. And you get into that bathroom this minute and get everything off. Fiancée indeed, wet, snivelling thing.'

'Nastenka, I'm not a fiancée. I'm a wife.'

'What? What do you mean, a wife? You've had a proposal and accepted, if I understood you right.'

'That's right. And after that I became Ivan's wife. Then we went swimming in the Neva, that's it. In a week's time we're going away together to Chernobyl in the Ukraine. He works at the atomic power-station there. That's my future, what else is there to tell?'

'I see. And college?'

'Night-school. Or maybe not. The most important thing is that I have three little girls and then one boy. Or the boy first and then three girls. It's probably marvellous, having an elder brother. But three girls, that's definite. Like us. We'll call one Nina after Mam, the other two will be Anna and Anastasia. Ivan agrees.'

'No, no, this is just too much of I don't know what. Anna! Anna! Take your little sister and waltz off to Paris or Amsterdam or Notre Dame or Madagascar, just get her away from all these crazy adventures!'

Anna came in with a dressing-gown, threw it over Alenka's damp shoulders and led her into the bathroom.

'Come on, come on, monster. So, do they really call him Ivan?'

'Of course. I couldn't miss a chance like that could I? Ivanushka and Alenushka, get it?'

'Personally – no. I can't take any of this in,' announced Anastasia, seizing a cigarette and twisting it in trembling fingers.

Anna came back in and rummaged in the book-case.

'What are you after?' asked Anastasia. 'Not champagne is it, to celebrate the triumph of permissive upbringing?'

'No, I've got no champagne. There was half a bottle of dry white somewhere though.'

From the bathroom came sounds of a shower going then Alenka singing, interrupted by a shout:

'Nastenka! Annushka! Even though you're clever and I'm an idiot, I still love you very much and I always will!'

14

CHAPTER 1

Anna, Sven and Faina hear the news

'Annushka! Time to get up! Coffee, tomato juice and mushroom omelette await you – and Sven with some new translations.'

Mm, what a way to start a new day! Anna smiled and opened her eyes. She'd never woken up anywhere so easily as here in Stockholm. It was most likely the Baltic air having this effect, the breeze from the dear familiar Baltic – and when had she ever been woken up by coffee in bed?

'Thank you dear Faina Borisovna. Good morning.'

Anna took the coffee cup in one hand and the glass of tomato juice in the other. The coffee gave her energy and warmed her up, the juice was refreshing. In two minutes all trace of sleep had vanished.

Having dressed and showered, she went down the cheerful wooden staircase with its squeaky treads and into the kitchen.

'Hi, Sven.'

'Hi, Anna. Sleep well?'

'Wonderful. I did dream I was lecturing to some people but I can't remember what about.'

'You're just keeping to the schedule Faina's laid down for you.'

Anna could never get used to the way Sven, who had been a pupil of Faina Borisovna and now worked with her as colleague and co-author of several books of translations, always called her just by her first name, Faina. What if one of Anastasia's senior pupils were to call her Nastya!

15

Democratic of course, but impossible. A touch of sadness came briefly to her at the thought of her sister, but Anna never gave in to sentimental musings on the past. Seven years since their parting, seven years without a single letter from either Anastasia or Alenka. One wasn't allowed to write because of her party, the other because her husband worked at an atomic plant. Forget it.

Besides, she felt warmed to the core by dear Faina Borisovna. It was a good thing she'd agreed to do a Swedish lecture tour; all of a sudden she'd meet with a person she could grow fond of and love, someone who could be a soulmate. In some way Faina Borisovna reminded Anna of her mother: the same gay readiness to find something to be pleased about whatever happened, like a child – a sunny day, a pretty dress, a neat witticism. Among the calm unhurried Swedes she blazed like a meteor infecting everybody and everything with her energy and carrying them along with her as she passed. Her aim was a noble one: in Stockholm it was really just around her that there existed this island of attention directed towards Russia, its literature and art. Faina Borisovna had left the Soviet Union more than twenty years before with her Swedish husband who used to joke: 'Sweden has no volcanoes, well, so I brought one back from Russia!'

While Anna was thus musing, Faina Borisovna was clattering the crockery in the kitchen, humming something and talking to Sven at the same time.

Anna studied the table and sniffed, rabbit-like:

'What's that marvellous smell? What else is there for breakfast apart from Sven?'

'Mushroom omelette with avocado.'

'Rather exotic!'

'Not more than your coffee and tomato juice, Anna,' smiled Sven.

'Coffee with tomato juice is my personal contribution to Western civilization.'

'Not the lectures and articles on samizdat poetry then?'

'No, just the coffee and tomato juice. Anybody can give lectures, but this – was an illumination, it really was, like a thunderbolt. The moment I realized you could mix my two

16

favourite drinks, I understood what a genius feels when he discovers something completely new in art. I felt like Mozart.'

'Not Mendeleyev? It is chemistry after all.'

'Einstein. It was a transformation of matter.'

'Get a move on, children,' Faina Borisovna broke in. 'The women's magazine writer is due in five minutes. Incidentally, Anna, have you got Irina's photos handy?'

'That's the packet on the refrigerator. I got them ready yesterday.'

'Splendid. What have you got for us today, Sven?'

'I've translated this one, here.'

'No, read it aloud Annushka, in Russian, then Sven can read it in Swedish. I can pick out anything by ear, I've got a perfect ear, as you know, children! If I read it myself I'm bound to get distracted by my own associations, my own thoughts get in the way somehow.'

'They would! Faina thinks at computer speed – and she never stops. Read, Anna.'

Anna picked up the paper, read it over to herself – for the nth time! Then aloud:

> In the half of the world I live in
> Skies are blazing with tails of comets.
> In the half of the age I live in
> Half the world strikes my eye in brightness.
> In my half a high wind is blowing
> And plague-feasts are held beyond number.
> But the searchlight plays on our faces
> And erases the trace of death's finger.
> And our madness goes drifting from us.
> And our grieving goes passing through us,
> And we stand at our fateful juncture,
> As our shoulders delay plague's onset.
> We will counter it with our bodies,
> We will march out against the nightmare.
> It will never get past – don't worry
> In the other half of the planet!

Anna stopped and put the paper down. Sven then read

17

the verses in Swedish. Faina Borisovna listened, nodding her head in time as if listening to music. Anna tried to catch from the intonation whether Sven had really felt the poem in the right way. Had he repeated the mistake of the French translator in imagining a conviction in it which Anna could not hear? He had put special emphasis in his translation on that 'we will counter it', 'it will never get past', 'don't worry'.

Anna wanted the West to hear something else: the frail shoulders striving to hold back the plague, that tiny woman with the curly hair valiantly standing in the path of the death-dealing wind. And in that 'Don't worry in the other half of the planet' she heard the bitter implication: if you don't want to hear us, if you want a quiet life, at least remember that we have nowhere else to go, the fearful stars already burn above our heads, the nightmare encloses us on all sides – and we will shield you, we simply have no choice. 'In my half, wind and plague.' But it was a plague of a different sort the wind was bearing now ...

Faina Borisovna liked the translation and it was decided that she would read it in Gothenburg along with others of Sven's translations.

'I liked that poem for another reason,' said Sven. 'It's dedicated to someone in the West – "my unknown friend David MacHolden", that means to all of us. It's a poem that forces you to think.'

'Well go on and think then! It seems to me the West isn't all that ...' Anna couldn't hold back.

Sven was somewhat hurt. It annoyed him when hints of a mature person condescending towards a child began to sound in Anna's voice. And of course it annoyed him that although he was Anna's age, she regarded him as no more than a boy, a child even. Also he was in love with her and had been for ever so long, three whole weeks, ever since her arrival in Stockholm. He yearned to stand guard over her, protect her and shield her from adversity. But these tiny Russian women were so full of daring, proud to suffer, head up, whatever fate had in store – they were even prepared to shield the whole world from plague with their own bodies! Sven had tried in his translation to express what he saw in Anna: the despairing resolve of a frail creature to take upon herself the full horror of death, shielding the rest of the world, unthinking in its foolish happiness. Well, let the Western world hear that desperate resolve, a wise Russian woman's bitter love. Then perhaps that world would want, like Sven himself did, damn it, to feel itself a man and take its stand if not in front, then alongside those who were taking the force of the plague-wind.

'Where's that reporter got to?' Faina Borisovna broke the silence. 'We'll be late for the train. We've got to leave inside forty minutes to get the nine-thirty. There's a reporter from a religious magazine catching it with us, he'll be interviewing Anna on the journey.'

'Is he from Gothenburg then?'

'No, Stockholm. He's getting the first train back from Gothenburg, there was just no other time to fit him in.'

'Good thinking,' Anna laughed. 'Interview at breakfast, interview on the train. Where else today?'

'Nowhere else. Two lectures in Gothenburg, then the train and back to Stockholm tonight. Sven's going to meet us and ferry us home. And show you his latest translation. There'll be nothing for you to do today Sven, with no us, so you can try and do another of Irina Ratushinskaya's.'

Anna smiled: Faina Borisovna could get everybody hard at work. In these last three weeks he had translated, as well as Ratushinskaya, three fine Leningrad woman poets – Ignatova, Schwartz and Pudovkina and some by those formerly published in samizdat and now living in emigration – Gorbanevskaya and Vladimirova.

'What are you working on now, Svenchik?'

'Liya Vladimirova's G-minor symphony.'

'Ah, how does it go ...'

'I've brought some Mozart for you here, I'll come back within the hour.'

Sven continued:

> He didn't come back in an hour,
> He didn't come back in a day,
> He didn't come back in a year,
> He never came back any more ...

19

There came a ring at the door. Faina Borisovna went to open it and returned to the kitchen with a young slip of a girl reporter accompanied by a hefty photographer, festooned with cameras and carrying a suitcase. Anna frowned slightly: why photograph her when she had so many photos of Irina Ratushinskaya?

Faina Borisovna chided her a little for being late.

'Oh, I'm so sorry! I stopped in to the office on the way to pick up a photographer and everybody was on about the latest news. Have you heard yet?'

'No we haven't had the radio on. What's happened?'

'Increased levels of radiation have been registered in this country. It's being suggested that the wind is bringing it in from the Soviet Union.'

'My God!' Anna exclaimed. 'All that talk about nuclear disarmament and they've gone and exploded something themselves.'

'Norway and Finland have also registered rises.'

'Have they asked the Soviet authorities?'

'See them admitting anything,' Faina Borisovna snickered. 'Those gangsters ...'

'No, the Soviet Union denies any increased radiation within their borders. The weathermen have confirmed that the winds have been from the direction of the USSR for the last seventy-two hours. They suspect some kind of atomic accident.'

'There's your "plague-wind" for you.' Anna sighed. 'It's probably from the north, there's an atomic submarine base there and loads of rockets. My father was killed there during tests on Novaya Zemlya. Secret tests.'

'No, they say the wind's been from the south of European Russia.'

'The south? That's odd. What could it have been?'

'No use guessing, Anna. On the way to the station we'll buy the paper and read it for ourselves. Now let's get on with this, we're very short of time.'

The girl-reporter seated herself opposite Anna and opened her notebook, the photographer already prowling round the kitchen, testing the light and choosing his angles...

The Central Committee of the CPSU, the Council of Ministers, the All-Union Central Council of Trade Unions and Central Committee of the Komsomol have summed up the nationwide communist voluntary day of overtime, in honour of the 116th anniversary of the birth of Lenin. It was a glowing testimony to the political and economic activity of Soviet people, their aspiration to respond in deed to the decisions taken at the XXVII Party Congress and to play their part in accelerating the socio-economic development of the country.

Radio Moscow, 26 April 1986, 11–00

New concrete houses have been constructed in Markelovo village in Tambov province.

Radio Moscow, 26 April 26 1986, 12–00

Forestry officials in Karelia began work today on assignments officially set for June.

Radio Moscow, 26 April 1986, 12–00

An agricultural fair has been taking place in one of the central squares in Kiev. Our correspondent reports.

Radio Moscow, 26 April 1986, 22–00

The Central Committee of the CPSU, the Praesidium of the Supreme Soviet and the Council of Ministers offer heartiest congratulations to the leaders of the Afghanistan Democratic Republic and the entire Afghan people on the occasion of their national holiday, the eighth anniversary of the April revolution.

Radio Mayak, Moscow, 26 April 1986, 14–00

Today Soviet sailors of the missile-cruiser *Vice-Admiral Drozd* on a routine visit to the port of Tripoli, have paid tribute to the memory of Libyan citizens who perished in the barbarous American bombing-raid of April 15th. Wreaths were laid on the grave of the victims.

Radio Mayak, Moscow, 26 April 1986, 22–00

When we say 'Nothing is forgotten' we are not prompted by the spirit of revenge but rather that of justice and concern for the future of all peoples, concern that no one should repeat such appalling evil. It is this which compels us to return again and again to the unmasking of Hitlerite crimes and to reminders of the lawful end of the fascist regime.

'The Fortieth Anniversary of the
Nuremburg Trials'
Red Star, 26 April 1986

The XXI Congress of the socialist united party of Germany, took place during its fortieth anniversary celebrations. The party rendered great service during the formation of the GDR. The theory of scientific socialism is being successfully put into practice in the centre of Europe, the homeland of Karl Marx and Friedrich Engels.

Pravda, 26 April 1986

CHAPTER 2

Anna thinks about Sven, her sisters and a good deal else

At last Faina Borisovna's energies began to flag; she put her feet up on the seat opposite and dozed. There was no one else in the compartment and Anna relaxed, gazing pensively out of the window.

White nights, like at home... The further north and east they reached in their lecture trips, the nearer home they got, the more she sensed its existence somewhere close at hand. After crowded central Europe what a pleasure it was to rest the eyes on these unpeopled forests and mountains. Very very occasionally a lake would flash by with a settlement on the shore or a lone house among the trees. The houses too were like ours in Karelia, ochre paint, shutter-boards, granite foundations. An area of swamp swept by, covered in cloudberries. Nowhere in Europe had she seen cloudberries or her favourite cloudberry jam. There were plenty of bilberries in Germany, usually served up with venison or other forest game. You could get cranberries in special shops, but cloudberries... still there had to be something they were short of! It would be nice to come to Sweden when the cloudberries ripened, go and see Sven's parents in the country, live in the forest for a bit and pick berries. It had been seven years now since she'd had a holiday, who'd have thought she'd have to work so hard when she emigrated! Anastasia had tried to frighten her with the bogy of unemployment. That there certainly was, but not for Anna, alas. A holiday for her was either a lecture tour, or when she finished work in advance – an article, review or essay. In seven years Anna had travelled the length and breadth of Europe, visited America and Australia, but she had never once visited the smallest town in Germany on her own initiative: it was all invitations, all planned timetables. Never mind. When this official part of the trip was over she would have three days for the return journey; she could actually go to the country with Sven and get the plane back and still be in time for the summer Russian courses. She would be working alongside Faina Borisovna so if the worst came to the worst she could take over from Anna for a couple of days and merge their two groups. That's what would have to be done. If only...

Just what on earth had happened over there, at home? If there'd been a hint of something definite in the papers or on television, they'd have spotted it: Faina Borisovna had bought every newspaper ánd before leaving Gothenburg they'd managed to see the television news – nothing concrete: radiation was emanating from the Soviet Union and the Soviet Union replied to all questions that nothing was going on. It could be quite a few years before the truth came out. They'd kept quiet about the explosion on Novaya Zemlya as long as they could. Later they admitted it to the West, but their own citizens to this day had no notion of the horror that had taken place, how many people were affected and were still ill and dying even now. If her father hadn't been killed on Novaya Zemlya, Anna wouldn't have known anything either. Well all right, now everybody would see what Gorbachev's talk about openness really amounted to. Quite the dissident with his openness. God! If he really wanted that, he'd find himself next day where they put people who want public accountability.

From Gothenburg, Faina Borisovna had phoned Sven, reminding him to meet them. Dear, naïve Sven it turned out had gone off to the press-centre after seeing them off that morning and looked through all the Soviet newspapers from the last three days, hoping to find some sort of information about the source of the radiation. Poor lamb, he'd been washing his hands ever since: after you handle Soviet newspapers for an hour, you're two hours getting yourself clean. And they have the nerve to talk about the 'dirty bourgeois press'. Anna recalled once buying the *Literary Gazette* at Frankfurt station on her way to Paris. Once in the compartment she threw it into the rack above her head and for a long time couldn't make out why her travelling companions were wrinkling their noses and covertly glancing at her. In the end, she picked up the paper herself; it literally stank of printers' ink. She had to look the thing through in the corridor and get rid of it to avoid stinking out the compartment all the way to Paris.

Still as soon as we get to Stockholm we'll have to get Radio Moscow – who knows, maybe Gorbachev's open policy might be working...At times the thought flitted across her mind – what if? Even the top leadership has to realize in the end that you couldn't fool the people all the time, you'd end up fooling yourself. Sometimes it seemed to her that the lot of them over there, in the Politburo, even if they didn't believe their own propaganda, had no grasp of reality at all. They just went through the motions like squirrels in a cage scared of jumping off their wheel in case it stopped suddenly. Oh, damn them. If only she could find out what had happened. If she'd been living at home she would hardly be so worked up; it's just that now, from here, life seemed so hard over there – and yet she'd lived the same life herself, she'd seen hard times and survived. And then the small joys of life, the day-to-day concerns pushed into the background that oppressive sense of living in a sick society, a country almost dying on its feet. From here, from afar that is, everything loomed larger, seemed more significant, much more definite – and much graver. When she lived at home she had never indulged in self-pity and didn't know how, she'd learned that from Anastasia. From here though, even her own life she sensed in her heart as a kind of tragic symphony in which any bright notes served only to show up the pervading mood of tragic hopelessness. Faith in God, faith in one's friends and faith in oneself, that's what kept them going at home. How little light there had been, how little joy, and youth was already gone, *that* music was fled. As fate had turned out, she had a second life to live, the question was, how? Seven years had gone by in a flash: nothing nowadays moved her to the

25

depths of her being, the flowers didn't smell the same, the trees had different names. Her spirits were easy – she had emerged unscathed from the pressures of her conscious Soviet years and could spread her wings now in freedom. Anna couldn't explain to Sven, or to any of her Western friends, just what freedom was: you couldn't explain what water in the desert meant to someone who had lived their whole life on the bank of a wide deep river. He would listen, nod, sympathize but what would he take in? It was freedom alone which fuelled her now; it certainly wasn't force of will or a sense of duty which made her work tirelessly. The same things at home had taken so much effort, both moral and physical, that now she moved easily from one task to another and from one type of work to another; if anything tired her at all, it was the multiplicity of impressions and new faces. That and the endless talk, her own as well as others'. Back home it had always gone without saying somehow that you should only talk seriously or at length with close friends or the friends of friends. You could only speak of what lay nearest your heart to people who were tried and true. But here you could be taken to visit people and inside half an hour somebody would say: 'Don't you get homesick? Do you miss your sisters?' And if you did, what would they do about it – take a tourist trip to Leningrad or Chernobyl and bring her word from her sisters?

Anna sighed and attempted to divert herself from these gloomy reflections. Really she wasn't being fair. It was a trial sometimes being with people, a careless word about the home she had left did hurt her, but she could hardly blame them – they couldn't possibly realize fully that she would never ever see her sisters, her home or her home town again. You might just as well ask a German in Australia whether he missed Germany. He would look a little sad and come out with some touching story no doubt – still what a difference there was. Maybe the previous year he hadn't saved enough money and this year his wife had wanted a holiday in Hawaii, but he knew that next year he could buy himself a ticket on a charter-flight and go off to his beloved Hamburg or Kamburg, the sea or the mountains he had

26

cherished all his life. And wasn't it marvellous, people around her living a normal existence and therefore unable to comprehend her sadness? Let them stay that way. She was, after all, working for them as well, and concerned for them in her attempts to get across the tragic meaning of that other existence.

However hard she tried, one set of cheerless thoughts replaced another. Some obscure urging kept bringing her back again and again to the comparison between her past and present lives as if some new unimagined change were imminent, something complex and testing forcing her to think, decide and choose. But what could possibly happen to her now? Fall ill perhaps, say she should die even. These things had ceased to worry her long ago: pain she had learned to endure and death held no terrors; it was, after all, only a transition from one life to another, from the familiar to the unknown. She'd already lived through something of the sort when she flew across the Soviet border, and in part before that even when she hadn't broken during questioning and so made her own choice – the camps. The camps were another world as well, so that meant she had passed through three worlds. Was she supposed to be afraid of some fourth dimension?

She regretted never having mastered the knack of sleeping on trains, she would love to have been able to curl up in a ball just like that and doze off wrapped in vague, warm thoughts. About Svenchik, perhaps. Lucky Faina Borisovna purring sweetly away there. Once upon a time Anna had enjoyed falling asleep to the clack of wheels and the rocking of the carriage. The trains here fairly slid along the rails, like a yacht through water, back there the carriages rolled from side to side, rumbling and jumping over the points. A specialist had told her that the railway lines in the Soviet Union had worn out long ago and were now beyond repair. The whole system had to be rebuilt from scratch. Still it had been wonderful sleeping to that click-clack long, long ago. When she was young that is, and later too. That was before the two months in a stolypin, the coach they transported prisoners in, a prison-carriage where guards patrolled the corridors day and night, in front of the

27

cages of the cell-compartments. The smell of railway oil, dust, sweat, urine, the sickening smell of herring and the ceaseless groaning pleas: 'Water!' It was hell trying to sleep in a stolypin and dangerous too: the wild northern and Siberian escorts usually drank the whole way and once they had a skinful, started pestering the women. Since that time Anna had lost the knack of sleeping on trains and the most luxurious trip meant for her exhaustion and insomnia, in every coach she smelt the whiff of the stolypin.

Well anyway it would soon be Stockholm; the familiar fiords lay beyond the window. Time to rouse herself and wash her face or what would she be like when Sven met them?

'Faina Borisovna, darling! Wake up, soon be Stockholm.'

Occasionally, when openness is spoken of, one hears the view that we should not be too hasty in exposing our failings and omissions. There can only be one answer to that, the Leninist one: 'For communists, always and under all circumstances, the truth is essential.'

Pravda, 26 April 1986

BUSINESSMEN, TOURISTS!
Aeroflot is reintroducing regular flights on routes Moscow–New York–Moscow from May 4th and Moscow–Washington– Moscow from April 29th.
MOSCOW AWAITS YOU! AEROFLOT

Moscow News, 26 April 1986

Reader Kutayev draws attention to poor behaviour on the part of a number of foreigners working in the Soviet Union and raises the question of a stricter attitude towards the violation of Soviet laws by foreign citizens. There have been quite a number of similar letters received.

Soviet Russia, 26 April 1986

Many Tashkentians will of course recall that April morning twenty years ago, April 26th 1966 when natural calamity struck our city. In a matter of seconds the earthquake had destroyed the majority of schools, agricultural establishments, hospitals and other buildings. Almost 100,000 families were left homeless. The entire country responded to the distress of our citizens and stretched out a helping hand; in a short period of time, the consequences of that catastrophic subterranean explosion were made good entirely. Over the last twenty years, the central area of the city, which suffered most in the earthquake, has been virtually rebuilt. And yet we have still a great deal more to do. It must be stated frankly that today Tashkent, a city of two million, has serious deficiencies in the provision of housing, sewerage, telephones and other city amenities. We have a great deal to do, and the most important is to increase productivity in building construction and improve the quality of residential accommodation.

Ernest Rezayev, first deputy chairman of the Tashkent municipal executive committee
Radio Moscow, 26 April 1986, 17–00

A powerful explosion took place today in Madrid city centre.

Radio Mayak, 26 April 1986, 12–30

Serious flooding has taken place in Argentina as a result of torrential rain.

Radio Mayak, 26 April 1986, 10–00

This autumn two states in Latin America suffered cruel natural disasters: Mexico a very severe earthquake, and Colombia a volcanic eruption. The whole world was informed of the number of victims. Central TV carried reports from the scene in every 'Time' news bulletin. However, on October 13th a powerful earthquake occurred in a number of areas in Tadzhikistan Republic. Apart from the words 'there have been casualties', no details were reported. And – not a single camera-shot on Central TV. Surely Tadzhikistan is nearer Moscow than Latin America is? So what's going on?...

Reader N. Khrapko, Primursky territory
Soviet Russia, 5 January 1986

CHAPTER 3

Sven meets Anna, tells her the news and is somewhat disappointed in her

Sven met them at the platform exit.

'Hi! How was the trip?'

'Marvellous!' cried Faina Borisovna, her eyes wide-awake and sparkling. 'Great success everywhere in every way! Anna got a bit overwhelmed with questions, that's all. She's out on her feet, poor lamb.'

'No, no, Faina Borisovna, I had a really good rest in the train. Has there been any news, Sven?'

'Oh yes indeed, amazing. Let's just get in the car and I'll tell you in order.'

In the car Anna sat next to Sven, apologizing to Faina Borisovna. The latter took this equably, acknowledging Anna's priority.

'Right, first. Do you know an emigré journalist called Oleg Tumanov?'

'Of course I do. I'm often in Munich and I've got friends there, I've seen Tumanov quite a few times round and about. I also know that he disappeared a month or two ago – what's he been up to?'

'Only that he gave an interview today in the Foreign Ministry Press Centre in Russia.'

'Oho, that is news. What did he do, repent of working for Radio Liberty and betraying the homeland?'

'Nothing of the sort. He just denounced the radio station he'd worked twenty years for.'

'He said it was a department of the CIA, no doubt.'

'Yes, it was basically that.'

31

'He didn't say how he suddenly turned up in Moscow?'

'The people who presented him talked about that. He applied to the Soviet embassy in a certain Western country, it seems.'

'Why do they say "a certain" I wonder. Surely it was in Germany since he lived in Munich.'

'Our reporters were all surprised they kept that quiet, but those were the very words: "in one of the Western countries".'

'There's no mystery,' announced Faina Borisovna. 'He applied to the Soviet embassy in London.'

'Why London in particular, Faina Borisovna?'

'Well, where else for heaven's sake? If he'd made up his mind to go back earlier he couldn't have chosen a better address. It was through London that Svetlana Alliluyeva went back, and Oleg Bitov and those poor boys, the prisoners from Afghanistan. It looks as if it's the London embassy that's got the job of sending lost Soviet sheep back home.'

'It's an odd coincidence, yes, I'd never thought of that before. But if he disappeared from the West such a time ago, why on earth have they just announced it? The Bitov announcement came right away, as I recall.'

'Looks like they interrogated him, getting him ready for the press conference, or maybe they were just waiting for a suitable moment. Anyway, they say he wasn't well briefed, he kept getting mixed up; the other Soviet representative had to keep answering for him, Arbatov.'

'Arbatov was there? Well now, that means they regarded this press conference as pretty important, I wonder why? And why choose this precise moment for his statement?'

'I wouldn't like to bet on it, but it could be there's a connection with the second news today. The press conference was two hours ago and two and a half hours ago TASS announced that there really had been an accident at one of the nuclear power-stations.'

'Aha! This time they've dropped in it!' shouted Faina Borisovna, thumping her fist against the back of the seat in front.

'Faina! Either I stop right there or you promise not to

terrify the driver, otherwise we'll crash into something.'

'Like a mouse, promise.'

'Well, go on Svenchik. Where's the power-station, did they say?'

'Yes. It's a hundred kilometres from Kiev. The town's hard to pronounce, Tshernopil, I think.'

'Chernobyl?!'

'That's right, that's how it sounded.'

'Sven, no!'

Anna pulled at Sven's sleeve, staring him in the face.

'Sven, you're mistaken, Sven you didn't hear it right, tell me!'

Sven hurled the car into the pavement and braked.

'Anna, what's the matter? What is it, Anna?'

Anna hugged herself round the shoulders and rocked to and fro, eyes closed.

Faina Borisovna embraced her from behind.

'Annushka, what's happened? Have you got a close relative near there?'

Anna, eyes still closed, replied in a crushed voice.

'My sister, Alenushka ... our youngest ...'

'Don't get too worried yet, Annushka, an accident isn't a disaster you know. Sven, what else do they say?'

'Two people killed, injured being treated, inhabitants being evacuated.'

Anna slowly turned her head.

'Evacuated?'

'Of course! I read it myself on the teletype. Take it easy Anna, love, it'll all be in the papers tomorrow I expect.'

'I can't just sit and wait till then, no I'm going to phone Anastasia. She's my elder sister. Before I left she made me promise not to write or phone, but this is different. Sven, can you get moving?'

Sven started the car at once.

Faina stroked Anna's shoulder.

'You're doing the right thing Annushka, we'll book a call to Leningrad straight away, find out what's going on and you'll feel better. I'm sure your sister's all right.'

'Oh if only I knew for certain where Anastasia was. She used to spend all the school holidays at our old flat in

Leningrad, but they could be repairing the school or I don't know what: or she's away on holiday somewhere. What if she's been visiting Alenka?'

'Anna, take it easy now, get a hold of yourself, this isn't like you. In an hour you'll know all about your sister, what's the point of worrying in advance?'

'That's not the point, Sven, we may not be put through.'

'What d'you mean not put through? You dial the code for Leningrad, your sister's number, and you speak to her, surely?'

'There's no automatic link with the Soviet Union, Sven.'

Anna's voice was cold, didactic.

'Why's that? You mean they have atomic power-stations but no automatic telephone system? I don't get it.'

'It's very simple. If there was automatic connection, how could they manage to control their citizens and decide who was allowed foreign phone-calls and when it was "inappropriate". In any case Sven, stop tormenting Anna with all these questions. You just do as she tells you, that's all.'

'Yes, yes, of course.'

And Sven lapsed into silence, not so much sulking as puzzled: of course there'd been an accident somewhere, possibly having some connection with Anna's sister living in those parts, but why the over-reaction? A funny lot, these Russians. Even Anna ...

Once in the flat, Anna rushed to the phone.

'You know the code, Anna?'

'I've phoned friends there from your place, I can remember it.'

She booked a call to Anastasia and settled down to wait as Faina Borisovna went out into the kitchen and started quietly rattling the tea things. Sven sat in an armchair wondering if it would be rude to leave before Anna spoke to Leningrad. He wasn't quite sure why he was sitting there anyway since he was serving no useful purpose and Anna had clearly lost her self-control and was exaggerating what had taken place.

Faina Borisovna emerged from the kitchen carrying a newspaper.

'Incidentally, there's some advice here about the

34

increased radiation in Sweden. Whole list of rules. Well, the dear Swedes are an obedient lot, they'll follow this to the letter. Tomorrow they'll all stop drinking milk, not go out so much, stop eating spinach, lettuce...'

Anna raised her head:

'If it's like that here, what must it be like over there?'

Sven shrugged.

'It's the right thing to do in the way of precautions, probably overdone. In the Soviet Union they'll have told everybody about anti-radiation precautions as well, stands to reason.'

Anna made no reply. Faina Borisovna smiled:

'Ah, Sven, you're a dear sweet boy! It might be just as you say in the Soviet Union, on the other hand it might be just the opposite.'

Sven heaved a small sigh. How politicized they both were ... you couldn't look at everything in the world purely politically. It was hard to imagine a government so idiotic as to conceal an impending danger like this from its own citizenry. It had to be said that in a crisis, if this situation could be called that, both Faina and Anna had fallen below his expectations. He felt a tinge of regret that Anna's heroic aureole was dimming for him, and her feminine charm with it; her behaviour was edging close to hysteria. Shame really...

Sven was never afraid to face reality. Sensing what was going on inside him, he resolved to stay and await the outcome of Anna's talk with her sister. To pass the time, he retrieved from his pocket the paper with the verses he had translated earlier in the day and began reading them through in a whisper, checking how it sounded once again.

'What's that?' asked Anna almost automatically. 'A new translation? Read the original.'

Sven raised his eyes to her, sighed and began reading the Liya Vladimirova poem:

> It's not a sorrow-stricken land
> That wakes a fleeting hour to pass –
> The final guilt is now at hand
> And looming over us at last.

And thistles, rooted in the dust,
Bloom along the ages' tracks;
A radiant God no longer trusts
Those darkened candles made of wax.

See the waves of incense roll,
The smoke of bonfires overhead...
Hear the bells in steeples toll –
But for the living, not the dead.

'That's speaking to the West as well, Sven.'

Anna said this flatly, without expression, the way she had been speaking for the last hour, but to Sven it seemed that even in her tense state she had noticed the process of disappointment taking place within him. 'Noticed but didn't comment', he thought sadly. Maybe it was better like this anyway. No words had ever been spoken between them, they could part in the same way.

The phone started ringing and Anna grabbed the receiver.

'Your call to Leningrad? Hold on.'

'Right.'

Faina Borisovna entered the room on tiptoe. 'Have you got through?' her eyes enquired. Anna shrugged in reply and started chewing her lip. The seconds dragged unbearably then suddenly ...

'Hallo?'

'Nastenka, is that you?'

'Hallo, hallo, yes, who's that?'

'Nastenka, it's me, Anna.'

'Anna!? Well, you have been a long time getting in touch. We'd already decided that Alenka and I'd dropped out of your life entirely.'

'But Nastya, it was you who told me never ...'

'Never mind that, you could have phoned or written.'

'Nastenka, just in case, jot down this number. Got it? Oh, Nastenka if only you knew ... how is Alenka?'

'Alenka's fine! She's got two lads, twins Antoshka and Aleshka. I'm going down to see them for a month to give Alenka a rest.'

36

'How old are they, Nastenka?'

'They're four already.'

'Good Lord! And where are they now, where's Alenka, where's her husband? How are things with them?'

'How should they be? Everything's fine. How are you getting on there?'

'I'll tell you later. Nastenka, you know something awful's happened, an accident.'

'What accident? What are you talking about?'

'Nastya, there's been a serious accident at the Chernobyl nuclear power-station. Two people killed, the radiation's got to Sweden ... Nastya! Nastenka! Hallo! Hallo! We've been cut off ...'

Anna put down the receiver. Sven and Faina Borisovna could hear the short, repeated notes clearly.

'I'll give it another try, if that's all right Faina Borisovna?'

'Of course, you've got to, maybe it just happened.'

Anna shook her head.

'Hardly. They cut us off just as I started to mention Chernobyl. You see, Sven, nobody knows anything about it over there. There might have been some announcement, who knows, but it could have been done in such a way that nobody would take any notice.'

Anna rebooked a call to Leningrad. This was accepted, but in half an hour the operator announced that 'the subscriber was not answering'. Anna then booked calls in turn to all her acquaintances in Moscow, Leningrad and Kiev. Faina Borisovna did the same to friends in various cities.

Both of them sat till morning, starting at every ring, but each time they heard the same thing: 'Subscriber is not answering, caller.'

'Miss, this is the tenth number I've tried, is nobody sleeping at home tonight?'

'Subscriber is not answering.'

Sven sat out the night on the sofa, tense, afraid of missing a word.

37

Comrade Zaikov, Politburo member and Secretary to the Central Committee of the CPSU commenced his stay in Tula province with a visit to one of the leading chemical plants in the country, the 'Nitrogen' industrial combine. He spent time observing many phases of production and met workers and specialists. His speech follows:
(Comrade Zaikov's speech)

Drillers of Main Tyumen Oil-Gas have completed their April target ahead of schedule.
(Story of drillers' successful month)

Kaluga agricultural workers are going ahead with cereal sowing and potato planting.
(Story of cereal and potato sowing in Kaluga province)

From the USSR Council of Ministers: An accident has occurred at the Chernobyl nuclear power-station. One of the nuclear reactors has been damaged. Measures are in hand to eliminate the consequences of the accident. The injured are being treated. A government commission has been set up.

In accordance with the agreement between the CPSU and the Spanish Communist Party, a Spanish delegation has been visiting the USSR to study party organization within the CPSU. The US Secretary of State Shultz has announced that the United States do not intend to desist from their terrorist activities directed against Libya...

Israeli invasion forces have taken over a further area of Lebanese territory...

The session of the Council of Ministers of the EEC has opened in Luxemburg. The community, as is well-known, is suffering the usual financial crisis at the moment...

CHAPTER 4

Anastasia seeks information
from the newspapers

Anastasia had been excited by Anna's phone-call, unexpected as it was and in the middle of the night too. She couldn't fall asleep again and made herself get up at six, her usual time, take a shower and do her exercises. After that she drank a cup of very strong coffee to brace her spirits. As she'd made the trip to Leningrad there was no point in wasting time: the library only opened today, so that's where she had to be. Then there was the shopping: some items for school, groceries, sausages and a bit of cheese for the Mayday celebrations, and if she was lucky and the queues weren't too long, a proper cake for the table. Somewhere along the way a bite to eat, and – the theatre. In the evening, the train home. Tomorrow the school parade and after that she would go and spend the evening with a friend, also a teacher, who would have baked some pies. Still a cake from Leningrad would be nice, they hadn't had a treat for a long time. That was why she'd kept on her Leningrad room in the share-kitchen flat, just so that she could come to town a few times a year and fill herself up with learning and culture. The room had turned into a haven for the other teachers in her school too as well as people seconded from the region: Leningrad hotels were always full to overflowing, so she gave keys to her village friends, region people and even to the friends of their friends. Of course these latter often got things for her; the school always needed something and the village couldn't always provide it. She had to pay for the room of course, and the telephone as well which she and her friends used about two months in the year. There was the gas and the light bill for the shared facilities as well as a bit to the neighbours for keeping things clean and tidy. There was another consideration preventing her from letting her room in the city: what if Alenka and her husband should take it into their heads to move to Leningrad? Or if not them, their sons. Once they grew up they might want to study in a big city, who knew what might happen? Today, she was glad that Anna had had somewhere to ring – the old house, the same number as when she was a child. Whereas if Anastasia had let the room, her emigré sister would have taken an age to find her...

Sitting at a table in the cool of the public library leafing through the last six months of *Family and School*, Anastasia recalled how her conversation with Anna had ended. What had she started to say about Chernobyl before they were cut off? Anastasia had been so excited by the mere fact of Anna's call after so many years apart that she hadn't paid attention to her last words. Some kind of accident at the nuclear plant? Well naturally there might have been an accident and those Western foul-mouths would have blown it up the way they do everything that goes wrong here. Still she'd better have a look in the paper just to make sure.

Anastasia handed in her magazines and headed for the newspaper hall. In that day's *Pravda* there were only Mayday items on the front page, but on page two in a lower corner she caught sight of a modest heading, 'From the Council of Ministers' above the following:

From the USSR Council of Ministers.
As already announced in the press, an accident has occurred at the Chernobyl nuclear power-station, situated 130 kilometres north of Kiev. A government commission is on the spot headed by the deputy chairman of the USSR Council of Ministers, Comrade B. E. Scherbina. The commission includes heads of ministries and departments, prominent scientists and experts.
Preliminary information indicates that the accident

took place in one of the buildings of No. 4 block and led to the destruction of part of the building housing the reactor, damage to which led to a certain leakage of radioactive material. The three remaining blocks have survived undamaged and are being held in reserve. Two persons perished in the accident.

Immediate measures have been put in hand to eliminate the consequences of the accident. At the moment, the radiation situation at the power-station and adjoining areas has been stabilized.

Medical treatment is being given to the victims. The inhabitants of the power-station settlement and the three closest areas of habitation have been evacuated.

The radiation situation at the Chernobyl plant and surrounding locations is being constantly monitored.

Anastasia read this and gasped: so that's what Anna had wanted to tell her, that's why she'd been asking about Alenka so excitedly. 'As already reported in the press' meant she had to look through previous issues. Why didn't they give the date of the accident? Anyway they hadn't said much of anything; the previous issues would carry fuller information.

She sifted through the papers but found no reference to the matter.

'Miss,' she called the librarian over. 'Help me please, I'm looking for some other information on this here – the accident at the Chernobyl power-station.'

The girl shook her head:

'I can't assist I'm afraid, there are no other items on that subject.'

'What do you mean, no? It's down here clear as can be: "As already announced in the press"...'

'I'm very sorry but there really is nothing in the central press. We've been looking specially through all the papers since morning, you're not the first one asking about it.'

'How can that be? ... It says so here in black and white. It's not any old item, it's a report from the Council of Ministers.'

'You know we even looked through the Ukrainian papers

41

and couldn't find anything. It's a mistake, most likely...'

'Miss! The people in the Council of Ministers don't make mistakes like that. If they write "As announced in the press" you have to look in the press for it, the central press at that! The Council of Ministers doesn't get banished to the regional papers!'

A rather short young man was listening-in to this exchange as he waited with his own enquiry. He touched Anastasia on the shoulder.

'Have you got relatives there or something, in Chernobyl? Why are you getting so het-up?'

'Why, what business is it of yours, young man? Well, yes I have got relatives there, my sister's family.'

The young man turned his head, distressed.

'You and your relatives have my sympathy.'

'Why, what on earth's happened and why should you sympathize?'

'Well, you know, I've heard this and that..'

'I don't need rumours. This is too serious, I want reliable information.'

'I'm not talking about rumours. Can I speak frankly?'

'Yes, of course, I keep telling you my sister's there.'

'Let's go out into the corridor then.'

In the corridor, they halted by a window.

'Well, I'm listening,' said Anastasia, impatient.

'You see, I just happened to be listening to the "Voice of America" the other day. They said that on the night of 26 April a major disaster took place at the Chernobyl nuclear power-station. There's been radiation as far as Scandinavia. There's evidence of a good many casualties.'

'Twenty-sixth, did you say? That can't be right, young man, today's the 30th...'

'There was a brief announcement on Moscow Radio on the 28th.'

'So you listen to Moscow Radio as well, not just "Voices"?'

'Yes, of course, and when I heard the news I rushed out to try and find something in the papers and since then I've been glued to the radio. There was one very short announcement, then nothing.'

42

'Then what about those words at the start of the report "As already announced in the press"?'

The young man smiled wryly:

'Maybe they're referring to the Western press in this case: all the papers there are writing up the story on the front page and they're printing advice to their own citizens on anti-radiation precautions.'

'Lord, what rubbish! What have they got to worry about?'

'Well, don't say ... A radioactive cloud drifted towards Europe, towards the north at first, then it moved south.'

'I don't know whether to believe you or not, but Western newspapers can't be believed ever. All right, let's stop there. Thank you for the information, but I'm going to try and get hold of it from my own sources.'

'Well, good luck.'

Anastasia followed the odd young man with her eyes; he reminded her of Anna, rather. Not just that he listened to 'Voices' ... but going up to a strange woman and letting it out that he listened to Western radio stations. It was clear as clear that it was on a permanent basis too – 'happened to' indeed. Was he really sympathizing or just bragging about how much he knew?

Anastasia made her way back to the newspaper hall and requested the *Pravda Ukraine* file. She examined intently every page of the 26–29 April issues, but nowhere was there any mention of the Chernobyl nuclear station. The 30 April number hadn't arrived at the library yet.

Anastasia returned the file, disappointed.

'Can one get foreign newspapers here as well, miss?' she asked.

'Which foreign newspapers? There are the communist ones, *Humanité* and ones like that. I'd be glad to let you have them but they're not available. They're being processed.'

'All right, give me the American papers. I know English. Let me have the ones where they write about the Chernobyl accident.'

'Excuse me but where have you been all this time?'

'I work in the province, at Svir. There's a river there, the

Svir,' replied Anastasia, trying to stop herself.

'Ye...es. No, we can only give out papers like that with special permission. We don't have any newspapers at the moment at all with anything about the Chernobyl accident. No papers for the last few days have come in yet for some reason. So I can't help you at all.'

Anastasia sighed, said goodbye and left.

The librarian, a serious young lady in glasses, stared thoughtfully after her. Her colleague came over and joined her.

'Why the deep thought, Natasha?'

'It was just that weirdo from Svir asking for "American newspapers".'

'Now that is weird! Did you ask her if she had special access?'

'No need, she obviously hadn't. Came from Svir ... You know, Ninochka, you listen to people and look around you and you get to thinking: why not chuck all this in and get the hell out of it somewhere, Svir or wherever, well away from here anyway. Live out in the country, teach kids and think you have the right to read American newspapers if you have a mind to.'

Decree of the Praesidium of the Supreme Soviet of the USSR
For outstanding industrial success and substantial personal contribution to the construction of the township of Pripyat and the bringing into operation of its energy capacity, the chief executive in charge of the building of the Chernobyl nuclear power-station for the Ministry of Energy and Electrification, Comrade Vasili Trofimovich Kizime is accorded the title of Hero of Socialist Labour together with the Order of Lenin and the 'Hammer and Sickle' gold medal.

President of the Praesidium of the Supreme Soviet of the USSR, K. Chernenko; Secretary to the Praesidium of the Supreme Soviet of the USSR, T. Menteshashvili
Moscow, Kremlin, 14 September 1984

Gazette of the Supreme Soviet of the USSR 38, 1984
Work on increasing the productive capacity of Chernobyl nuclear power-station goes ahead. The fifth and sixth blocks should go into service in 1986 and 1988. With the commissioning of these blocks, the station's capacity will reach 6 million kilowatts making it the most powerful in the world ... Construction work should go forward without interruption on the basis of the strictest observance of building techniques. But that is just not happening. The problems associated with the first block have gone on to the second and third and so on and what is more have grown in the process, accumulating an enormous number of unsolved difficulties. Block five: [...] Poor quality of design paperwork has necessitated extra work, alterations and expenditure of material and moral effort. The inability of engineering and technical personnel to organize the work schedules of the construction gangs has led to a lowering of expectations. 'Exhaustion', the wearing-out of equipment, machines and mechanical appliances, shortages in mechanization, specialized instruments etc. have begun to tell. In short, all the faults of the construction mechanism, typical, alas, have begun to

show themselves in an acute form. Now, of course, measures are being concerted to normalize the position but time has been lost [...] In citing these facts, I wish to focus attention on the inadmissibility of shoddy workmanship in the construction of atomic power-stations. Every cubic metre of reinforced concrete should be a guarantee of reliability, and consequently of safety. The chief guide for anyone taking part in the construction of energy installations must be, first and foremost, his conscience.

Lyubov Kovalevskaya,
Literary Ukraine, 27 March 1986*

At the moment, no one can give a final answer to the question of what caused the accident at the Chernobyl nuclear power-station [...] Undoubtedly the most convincing fact in favour of the basic reliability of RBMK-1000 reactors† is the faultless performance of the other ten reactors of this type in other Soviet nuclear power-stations. The first of these, moreover, began working at the Leningrad station as long as thirteen years ago.

APN, 22 May 1986

---

*A month before the disaster (J.V.)
†The type which blew up at Chernobyl (J.V.)

CHAPTER 5

Anastasia makes enquiries of a senior party comrade

Anastasia emerged from the library and crossed the road into the little square in front of the Pushkin Theatre. She sat down on a bench in front of the statue of Catherine the Great and was soon deep in thought.

People wandered past, children played in the sand-pit, an old woman next to her was knitting and a young man read the paper. And nobody, nobody at all had an inkling that perhaps at that very moment among those cheerful swirling clouds above their heads, there sailed one particular cloud, different from the others, bearing disease and destruction to them all. Could she believe some dissident youth and his information sources, those hostile radio voices? No, she mustn't give in to alarm just like that, she couldn't put any trust in that sort of information. It was perfectly possible that enemies abroad were deliberately sowing panic via their 'listeners'. The nuclear station near Leningrad, in Pinewoods, had been in operation since 1973 and that was all right, no danger. She remembered Ivan saying that the reactors at Chernobyl were of the same type. Anyway Anastasia wasn't alone, she had just felt like that in a moment of weakness. She had her party colleagues, that's who she should be talking to! First though she should try and find out what she could herself. What was she doing dropping her hands and snivelling all over the place!

'I really am stupid,' she called aloud, so that people sitting next to her on the bench looked at her, astonished.

'I've just got to book a phone-call to Alenka, that's all there is to it!'

The taxi rank was at hand, but there was a fair-sized queue, so Anastasia took a trolleybus to the Petrograd side.

The telephone booking was accepted, but an hour passed, then another and no ring came. She contacted inter-city again and got the reply: 'There's no connection available and won't be today. There's damage to the line. We're cancelling the booking.'

Of course, that's probably what it was, the line could be damaged without there having been an accident at all. There were dozens of reasons for damaged telephone lines. And yet she felt herself growing still more anxious.

She smoked her way through papirosa after papirosa, pacing up and down, thinking furiously. If she did nothing and waited till Alenka rang her, she could go quietly mad. She'd already abandoned any thought of holiday presents or the theatre as well as the history text-book she'd actually come to Leningrad for – it wasn't for the cake!

What on earth could she do, what could she do now? Tomorrow was the holiday, tomorrow she assuredly had to be at school and that meant being in the dark: there'd be nothing in the holiday newspapers. She wasn't going to spoil anybody's Mayday. If she only knew that it would occur to Alenka to phone her at school, she could wait in her study. She had to be at the parade, of course – a Mayday parade without the headmistress was unthinkable, the last parade for the school-leavers too. Her speech was already prepared. Why hadn't she managed to get them to put a phone in her school house? Though she spent so little time in the place, it hadn't entered her head somehow: she was at work the whole day and had the telephone close at hand. Alenka always phoned in the mornings, before the start of the school day – she knew that was the only time, when Anastasia wasn't being besieged in her study, when she had five minutes for a quiet chat. No, Alenka would never think to phone tomorrow morning, there wasn't a hope of that. And anyway, where was she? They'd said in the report that the power-station personnel had been evacu-ated. It was a pity she'd never stirred herself to go and visit

48

Alenka: so now she had no idea whether she actually lived near the actual plant or not. The main thing was how extensive the damage had been. How could she find out?

Anastasia thought and thought and finally concluded that she would have to apply to Valeri Ivanovich for help. If only he was at Smolny now and hadn't gone off on vacation or Mayday celebrations somewhere. Come to think of it there was a demonstration on Palace Square that evening, so that he was bound to be back for that. Also she had his home number with her. One thing going for her at least.

She rang Smolny first, but she was told that Valeri Ivanovich was at a conference and wouldn't be returning to Smolny that day. She then rang the home number. Luckily it appeared he had come back from the meeting and lain down for a while; his voice was rather sleepy, not properly awake.

'Valeri Ivanovich, this is Anastasia Nikolayevna Lebedeva.'

'Ah, my dear, hello! Glad to hear your voice. Well, how are things on the rural fields of enlightenment?'

'Everything's fine at school Valeri Ivanovich.'

'I'm sure of that. Your school is our pride and joy. So what's the problem – after something else for the school and need my help? We'll help, we surely will. Let's wait till after the holiday; then come directly to me and tell me all about it.'

'Valeri Ivanovich, it's a personal matter.'

'Personal? Ah, I've got it! You want a seat on the rostrum? You'll have it, I promise my dear. Many another I'd refuse but you are worthy to be among the cream of the people of the city and province, an equal among equals. What's more, I'll fix an interview for you with *Leningrad Pravda* or the radio. So everything all righty? Go straight along to Smolny this minute and get your invitation from my secretary. I'll ring her right now.'

'Valeri Ivanovich, I ...'

'Now, now, no thanks necessary, no. I'll see you on the rostrum tomorrow. My best regards.'

The receiver indicated that he had hung up.

Exasperating! What on earth now? Anastasia had realized

after the third word that Valeri Ivanovich had had a few, he wasn't tired or sleepy. Ring him again to explain herself? Would he understand – and he might lose his temper. Refusing a rostrum seat now would be embarrassing – such an honour too. Well, nothing to be done. Now she would go along to the party provincial committee for her ticket and try to get to him tomorrow and sort it all out. At school they'd get by without her somehow.

At Smolny, Anastasia received further confirmation of Valeri Ivanovich's benevolent attitude towards her. Apart from the rostrum ticket, the secretary had arranged for her, at his request, a pass to a restricted shop where she stocked up with good-quality smoked sausage, fresh cucumber and a box of fancy pastries for the holiday. Now she needn't race round the shops and jostle about in queues. Back home she thrust all these luxuries in the fridge, the only expensive object in the whole room. It had been bought, in fact, with these food safaris to Leningrad in mind.

Anastasia didn't go to the theatre: the Mayday demonstration was due to start early; the streets of the city were being closed off by police. That meant she had to get up early next day and that in turn meant an early night tonight.

She slept fitfully however, and her dreams were filled with alarms.

Guests and party hierarchy were of course seated separately on the rostrum, and Anastasia would have been hard put to it to reach Valeri Ivanovich; he remembered her himself, however.

'This way, if you please!' He appeared unexpectedly alongside her, accompanied by a sprightly young miss with a camera and tape-recorder. 'This is our village school headmistress, hers is one of the top schools in the province. Let me introduce you!'

The young miss switched on the tape-recorder and started chattering glibly, that here was a village school headmistress standing on the dais for honoured guests looking up into the blue sky and thinking ...

'What are you thinking about, Anastasia Nikolayevna, looking up into the blue Mayday sky?'

Anastasia glanced into the sky. It really was blue.

'You're thinking about peace, aren't you? That the sky above the planet should always stay blue like this?'

Anastasia gave a wry smile.

'Let's hope not! I live in a village, and I know that a sky that's always blue means a long drought.'

'Oh, that was just an example!' cried the girl, annoyed. She clicked at her tape-recorder. 'Let's do it again from the beginning. What are you thinking about ...'

Again she harped on about the blue sky. So as not to mess up someone else's work, Anastasia meekly wished all the earth's inhabitants a blue, cloudless sky. Recalling the Ethiopian drought, she nevertheless frowned. Still, what could you do, every job had its set ways – journalism included.

Detaching herself from the cloudless girl, Anastasia sought Valeri Ivanovich with her eyes. He hadn't got far and was anchored among a group of sturdy party members. Anastasia went up to him and touched his sleeve.

'Ah, Nastyushka! Well, today you'll be queen of the air-waves over all Leningrad if not the whole country.'

'Thank you, Valeri Ivanovich, but I'd like to talk to you on a serious personal matter!'

'Personal and serious as well. Not thinking of giving up country life, are you?' Valeri Ivanovich frowned slightly.

'Good heavens, no. No, this is something quite different. Valeri Ivanovich, you know the accident at Chernobyl nuclear power-station?'

'Well, I do know something ... but why bring that up on a holiday, my dear?'

'I'm sorry to go on about it today, but I've got relatives living at Chernobyl, a sister and her family, two little children. And I've heard nothing from them.'

'What were their jobs there? Where were they living?'

'In the settlement. He's a physicist working at the plant. There's been nothing from them, next to nothing in the papers, I'm going mad with worry.'

'No need to worry. Atomic accidents are no joke, so you can be sure that everything needful is being done. They'll find your relations, they'll have been evacuated along with the others, that's all. So don't worry yourself sick, enjoy

51

yourself. What a day for the holiday, eh? Just what the doctor ordered!'

'Valeri Ivanovich, I stayed in Leningrad for Mayday specially to find out something about Chernobyl. You are my only hope. There's nobody else here who can help, nobody else has such access to channels.'

Valeri Ivanovich was pleased by this hint of 'access'. He considered, chewing his full lips, and his face brightened once more.

'Yes, yes, I know, dear heart; there's someone who can explain all. Come with me ...'

He led Anastasia over to the party section of the rostrum, exchanging greetings with acquaintances as he went. He halted before a grey-haired man wearing large horn-rimmed spectacles.

'Right, Gennadi Borisovich can enlighten you on the subject of Chernobyl.'

Gennadi Borisovich and Anastasia were then introduced.

'May I ask why you're so interested in Chernobyl?'

'Well, her sister's there with her husband and children, so she's upset and worried; you can understand. She doesn't know quite how to cope, it's the first accident there's been at one of our power-stations, after all! You just calm our Nastyushka down. You're an atom specialist, aren't you?'

Gennadi Borisovich said nothing for a while. He then looked closely at Anastasia.

'Are you a party member?'

'Yes. Fifteen years now.'

'Can you keep a safe tongue in your head?'

'Of course.'

'Well then. The situation at Chernobyl is serious, very. The people there at the time of the accident aren't to be envied.'

'Were there casualties?'

'There were, and considerable discharge of radiation. The entire population have been evacuated and are undergoing checks. Where did your relative work?'

'In the power-station.'

'What as?'

52

'Operator.'

'Then I won't conceal it from you. You have every reason to be anxious. When the alarm went all personnel were called to the station, so he may well have received a dose. Yes, not a pleasant story ... But good for you, you didn't panic, you came to the provincial party for advice. That's the party thing to do. And I'll do my best to help you. We'll have to get the holiday over first, then come to me and we'll try and find out everything we can about your relatives.'

Anastasia thanked him, took a note of his phone number and made her way back to her place on the rostrum. She couldn't very well leave: Valeri Ivanovich might notice and take offence. She stood on the dais and watched the endless human river flowing past beneath her, automatically reading the repetitive slogans on red fabric and listening to the same blaring slogans on the radio. Their meaning had no power to penetrate now. Her head ached abominably, and overhead shone the cloudless sky.

CHAPTER 6

Anastasia delivers notes in Moscow

... Valeri Ivanovich, dear man, had put himself out to secure Anastasia a Moscow hotel room. Since morning she'd been busy going from one office building to another, equipped each time with a personal note to the appropriate individual. Gennadi Borisovich had given her a note for the Energy Ministry. She was told nothing definite there, but received a note to the Atomic Energy Committee. There she was informed that victims were being treated in Hospital No 6. The final note was addressed to Comrade Guskova, in charge of the Chernobyl accident ward.

Anastasia's arrival in Angelina Konstantinovna Guskova's office coincided with that of a group of Soviet journalists. She didn't feel like showing her note in public like this, or revealing her private concerns either, so she decided to sit out the conversation, trying not to draw attention to herself.

Angelina Konstantinovna, a middle-aged woman with large sunken eyes and deep creases around the mouth, at once adopted a most decisive manner with the journalists.

'Let's get things straight from the start. This is a special situation, our patients are in a grave condition. There are some whose lives we greatly fear for. So any word out of place, especially naming names in a sensitive context, could be extremely counter-productive. So no surnames, no prognosis.'

'Can we meet and talk to any of those not so badly affected?'

'Not under any circumstances.'

'Is that your own decision or orders from above?'

'Here I issue the orders.'

'And you can't give us a single name?'

'What on earth for? I'll tell you about our doctors and staff doing all they can to save those irradiated. We can talk about the American, Doctor Gale, with whom we have an excellent professional relationship.'

Angelina Guskova dominated the conversation; traps she saw at once and, other than generalities on courses of treatment, gave not a scrap of information. On the question of patient numbers her answers were brief and vague: around two hundred. They were the people who on the night of 26 April were in close proximity to the reactor.

'Can we talk to anyone else of the medical staff?'

'No. My assistants have a very heavy work-load at the moment. "Distribution" as follows: three shifts of doctors, four of nurses, there's a whole army at the disposal of the hospital administrator. That's why I'm requesting you reporters to keep away from my assistants: they are on constant bedside duty.'

'How do the patients get on with the American doctors?'

Professor Guskova smiled:

'When we warned out patients that American doctors would be coming for a look round, there was a very interesting reaction: well, let them come ... they have to learn as well. For us, that sort of thing is the highest praise.'

The reporters began to laugh and whisper among themselves. Anastasia was surprised at their reaction: what was so astonishing about Guskova's patients believing Soviet medicine to be in advance of American? Every schoolchild knew – everyone could read the paper nowadays.

Angelina Konstantinovna rose and indicated to the journalists that the audience was at an end and it was time for her to get back to work. Respectfully taking their leave and thanking her for an informative meeting, the reporters filed out one by one, taking the final photos as they did so.

Anastasia remained behind and Guskova looked at her interrogatively.

'You've got another question? I'm in a considerable

hurry, my patients are waiting.'

Anastasia handed over her note. Guskova read it through and glanced at her again.

'So what is it you want actually?'

'I would like to find out for certain if Alenka and Ivan Prikhotko are among your patients.'

'I've just told people in your presence, that we avoid mentioning our patients' names.'

'Ivan was an operator at the station. Are there any operators among your patients?'

'There are operators too, yes.'

'Are there any women?'

'Not many. Of the serious cases – two. Well, all right, I'll tell you: neither of them is called Alenka. Is that enough for you?'

'Well yes, something of a consolation at least. Thank you very much; I was hoping though that one of the less affected patients could tell me something of what happened to Ivan.'

'No, meetings are definitely not allowed here even for relatives.'

'Why? Are there medical reasons?'

'Those as well. Now we shall have to say goodbye. Good luck and I hope you find your sister well and unharmed.'

Anastasia left the study to find one of the assistants waiting to escort her to the exit in polite silence.

As already reported, two persons died and 197 have been taken to hospital, of whom forty-nine have been sent home after investigation.

USSR Council of Ministers
Pravda, 1 May 1986

Only personnel in close proximity were endangered. These were few in number since the Chernobyl nuclear power-station is a highly automated complex.

Georgi Arbatov, Director of the United States & Canada Institute
APN, 8 June 1986

Among the victims, eighteen are in a grave condition. There are no foreign nationals among those affected.

Radio Moscow, 2 May 1986, 9–00

As a consequence of the accident, two persons were killed, more than a hundred affected by radiation. All were transferred to Moscow on the night of 27 April.

A Kovalev, Deputy Foreign Minister USSR
Pravda, 7 May 1986

Two people were killed, one of them a fireman bravely grappling with the conflagration. A further 204 persons who were inside the contaminated zone have been hospitalized. A number of these have left the clinics after medical checks.

Igor Zaseda, Maxim Rilski
APN, 8 May 1986

As a result of the accident, two people were killed, 197 were taken to hospital of whom twenty are in a serious condition. Forty-nine however have been allowed to leave hospital after medical investigation.

Spartak Beglov
Moscow News, 11 May 1986

Thirty-five people are in a serious condition, six
persons who sustained burns and radiation have died.

USSR Council of Ministers
Radio Mayak, Moscow, 12 May 1986, 21–00

As of today, 299 persons have been hospitalized,
diagnosed as suffering from radiation sickness of
varying degrees of severity. Seven have died.

M. Gorbachev, speech on television
14 May, 21–00

I would like you to understand the following.
When it is reported: the patient is in a grave condition, it
means the crucial phase of radiation sickness has set
in, the destruction of the bone- marrow. After one or
two weeks it may return to normal. Therefore
information on the condition of a patient, which
accurately reflects the actual situation, may vary from
day to day.

Andrev Vorobyov, candidate member of USSR
Academy of Sciences
APN, 16 May 1986

Nearly 300 people were exposed to radiation levels of
varying intensity, some representing danger to life. It
proved impossible to save nine of these.

APN, 22 May 1986

In all, as of today's date, 187 people officially
diagnosed as suffering from radiation sickness are
being treated in the country's medical centres. In spite
of counter-measures and expert medical aid twenty-
four patients have died in this period.

O. Schepin. First deputy USSR Ministry of Health
Radio Moscow, 5 June, 20–30

Around two hundred patients were registered. About
seventy were allowed home. Some 120 have been
kept in hospital. Our hearts and minds are constantly
preoccupied with seventy to eighty of those.

Professor Angelina Guskova
Izvestiya, 28 May 1986

I would like to remind you that at Chernobyl, two persons died, not 2,500 as at Bhopal, and 200 people sustained radiation doses, not 100,000 as in India after the explosion at the American Union Carbide factory. Of those 200, incidentally, forty-seven have already left hospital.

Georgi Arbatov, *APN*, 8 June 1986

CHAPTER 7

Anastasia among the dissidents

Towards evening, Anastasia had exhausted her supply of
notes and resolved on a desperate step: she phoned Anna
herself from a trunk-call office. The receiver was picked up
by the flat-owner, a middle-aged woman, judging by the
voice. Anna was still in Sweden and was overjoyed to hear
her sister.

'Nastenka! Well, any news of Alenka? I'm going mad
with worry here.'

'No, nothing yet. I'm trying to find out something in
Moscow but I haven't got far yet. I'm afraid it might mean a
trip to Kiev. Are you going to be long in Sweden?'

'No, I'll be back in Germany soon. Write down my
address and telephone number in Heidelberg.'

Anastasia did so.

'Anna, I need another number. Remember you had a
friend in Moscow, the one who helped you such a lot after
'77.'

Anna exclaimed softly in surprise.

'Nastenka! ... OK, this is it.'

And she dictated the number of a man who, when Anna
was in the camp, used to come to see her, send her parcels
and even offered money to her sisters, though Anastasia had
turned that down, realizing that assisting political detainees
was against the law.

After she put the phone down, Anastasia dialled the
number at once.

'May I speak to Andrey Petrovich?'

'I'm afraid that's impossible, unfortunately. Andrey Petrovich is out of town.'

'When will he be back?'

'Four years' time.'

'Ah ... I see. I'm sorry ... only he could have helped me just at this moment.'

'Yes, there are quite a few saying that. And who are you , can you tell me your name?'

'You don't know me but you may just know my sister, Anna Lebedeva.'

'Annushka? Why of course! How is she? Is she writing anything? I'm Andrey Petrovich's wife.'

'We phone each other. Everything's fine with her.'

'Yes, and just why are *we* phoning? You're in Moscow, aren't you?'

'I am.'

'Well come over to us then. You can tell me about Annushka and whatever it was you wanted with Andrey Petrovich – perhaps I can help.'

'If it isn't too much trouble ...'

'Of course not.'

Anastasia jotted down the address and set off at once.

Andrey Petrovich's family lived in a newly built suburb. Their flat was modern but shared with neighbours. It was a neighbour who answered Anastasia's ring at the door. She gave Anastasia a malevolent glance:

'People coming and coming. One came to a bad end! Natasha! For you.'

A young woman with a babe in arms came out into the corridor.

'Anastasia Nikolayevna? Come through into the room.'

Anastasia followed her into a small, light room where two more children, a boy and girl of about eight or nine, were sitting at the table. The boy bore a strong resemblance to Andrey Petrovich from what Anastasia could remember of him from their several encounters: the same wavy hair and dark eyes. Yes, and there was his portrait over the writing-desk: thin, with a cheery, rather comical face. Come to that, do-gooding attracted the eccentrics; who else would do it?

'Natasha. If you need to talk you can go into the garden,

62

we'll sit with Vaska,' the boy offered. It seemed strange to Anastasia that he called Andrey Petrovich's wife by her first name. Well, of course, dissidents had their own way of carrying on.

Natasha gave Anastasia a meaning look:

'That's true, it would be nice to stroll about a bit. There's a lovely garden next to us. Coming?'

This business of inviting someone in and then taking them out for a walk struck Anastasia as odd.

Natasha handed over the toddler to the other children and went with Anastasia into the garden.

Once outside, Natasha asked:

'You realize why I suggested leaving the house? They're probably listening in and if I guess right you've got something important on your mind. It's safer out here.'

'Ah, I see now. I was surprised ... what happened to Andrey Petrovich then?'

'You're not with it at all, then?'

'No. I should let you know from the very start that I never had anything to do with my sister's dissident activities. I know Andrey Petrovich because I used to see him with Anna and then he went to see her in the camp and brought me messages; and he helped me to pack the parcels. I lived in the village you see, we had no condensed milk or decent tinned stuff. So that's how we got to know each other. He even offered me and my sister money but I wouldn't take it. I'm a headmistress and a party member, it wouldn't do. I've got another confession to make: I never approved of what Anna was doing. Not that I understand even now what your "democratic movement" really means. Still, I'm in such a weird situation that I've got nowhere else to turn.'

Natasha heard Anastasia out and nodded, understanding. Even her confession of hostility to their movement drew only a faint smile.

'Tell me all about it in order. What's this disaster that's happened to you? Maybe I can help – or if not me, somebody else.'

Trying to remain calm and not betray signs of panic, Anastasia related in order everything that had happened to

63

her over the last few days, from Anna's phone-call to today's fiasco with Professor Guskova.

After listening to all this, Natasha didn't bother to get worked up over the government's actions, or condemn those people who might have helped Anastasia. She considered deeply for a while, then asked:

'If you let me tell my friends all this, one of them might help you to trace your Alenka. I can't think of anything just at the moment. You read the papers and listen to the radio, that's one thing. This is living history ... so I can tell my friends all about it?'

'I've got no choice,' replied Anastasia simply.

'It means waiting till we find the right person. Are you staying at a hotel?'

'Yes.'

'That's terribly expensive isn't it? You know what, move in here with me. There's another little room here where the children sleep. We'll use the big one – and don't feel awkward about it, Anna was a good friend of the family. Perhaps you don't know this, but I get parcels from her. And not just me, she helps a lot of people from where she is.'

Anastasia smiled sadly: wasn't that just like Anna? Sending parcels to other people and not letting her own sisters know how she was. She had forgotten ordering Anna to cross them out of her life. Now after all that had happened it seemed to her that Anna should have acted differently; principles were principles but they were sisters, one blood when all was said and done. That was the main thing.

Anastasia agreed to move in with Natasha and within the hour had brought her things with her from the hotel. In the evening, Natasha's and Anna's friends gathered in the flat. There was much talk and argument, three kettles of tea disappeared and it was decided that everyone together would help Anastasia to find Alenka. The first thing to be decided was whether Alenka or her husband really were in Clinic No 6 in Moscow after all. If there was no trace of her sister in Moscow, Anastasia would travel to Kiev, where Natasha's friends would locate people who might help.

The day Anastasia spent with Natasha brought the world

of Anna's past closer to her. Previously all she had known was that Anna, proud and independent as she was, contemptuous of accepted norms and proprieties, had friends of her own way of thinking. What exactly they got up to, she had no desire to know. She had a rather vague picture of a party like her own, only in reverse: their own picked people, with their own aims, even their own privileges. From the help Andrey Petrovich had given to Anna that time, Anastasia had censoriously concluded that dissidents did pretty well on food parcels from abroad and that their activities, admittedly risky, were far from disinterested. That's what she heard, inevitably, at closed party meetings and the KGB investigator assigned to Anna's case kept on saying the same thing. Now she was witnessing something rather different.

Natasha got up every morning at half past five, got the children's breakfast, got Vaska ready and took him to a creche on the other side of the city, then back across town to where she worked. In the evening this journey was repeated, so that she was never home before seven and sometimes later. She had to do the shopping en route as well.

The older children got up and had their breakfast on their own. The boy, it turned out, was Andrey Petrovich's son from his previous marriage. During the investigation his first wife had categorically denied any connection with him and said a good deal more than she should. After the trial she had suddenly announced that she had no intention of 'rearing a son of an enemy of the people'. In actual fact, according to friends of them both, it was an opportunity for her to marry again and the child was a stumbling-block. She placed him in a children's home, much to the anguish of Andrey Petrovich when he somehow learned of it. It was then that Natasha took little Yura in herself. The mother agreed to hand him over, on condition that he was registered 'in his father's living-space' that is, in Natasha's flat, so Yura became Natasha's third child. As the wife of a political detainee she received assistance from the Solzhenitsyn fund but it wasn't enough to prevent them living in poverty. Amid all this, Natasha, worn out by work, the travelling from one end of the city to the other and the nightly darnings and washings, contrived to help the families of other detainees as if filling the place of her imprisoned husband. She and the children lived mainly on soup, milk, potatoes and porridge. Fruit was scarce, they rarely ate meat and if they had sausage or cheese it was of the cheapest. Yet Natasha's fridge was crammed with tins of stew and sausage-meat for the prisoners in the camps, along with smoked sausage and slabs of white chocolate from Switzerland. And even the children never laid a finger on any of these rare delicacies. It was the same with money: people came to the house with substantial sums and Natasha would retrieve an exercise book from its hiding-place, and mark and check among the coded contents before distributing the money to certain addresses that very evening. Once Anastasia heard someone advise her: 'You should go by taxi, that family's way over on the other side of Moscow.' 'You're joking – d'you know how much it costs?' replied Natasha, and took the tram. She came back late at night and almost overslept in the morning.

While Anastasia was there Natasha got a parcel from abroad. That evening friends gathered to discuss who should receive it.

'Chocolate, coffee, sweets – that's for parcels, but who should get the jeans? Which of us has got the raggiest backside?' enquired Natasha breezily.

'The raggiest backside' turned out to belong to a certain non-conformist artist who was immediately summoned by telephone to receive his jeans. Natasha, surveying the company, claimed only the children's shoes for herself.

'If there isn't anyone going barefoot and takes this size, can I have these for Vaska? You can't get children's shoes in the shops for love nor money.'

Out of all the varicoloured heap of foreign goods and clothing only these little shoes remained in the house. Also some chocolate for the elder children, this at the insistence of the guests and then only because one bar turned out to be brown chocolate, not white and so wouldn't have been allowed into the camps.

Ideas and attitudes aside, those little shoes trod a path

into Anastasia's heart. Seeing how Natasha was being torn apart between work, home and 'charity' – a word Anastasia still said to herself ironically, recalling Gorky's 'don't insult a man by pitying him' – she decided to discard the anxiety which had paralysed her up to now and assist Natasha about the house in some way. Apart from wanting to help, there was also a straightforward rational calculation: Natasha had freed her from the expense of hotel living, so she should in her turn pamper the children with fruit and fresh vegetables.

The Moscow market, however, reminded her again of Chernobyl. When she had bought her cucumbers, radishes, strawberries, even a bunch of flowers, and had actually left the market gates, she noticed a weeping woman with two huge baskets. She was surrounded by a group of grim-looking people. As she passed, she caught the words: 'Ee, I'm not from Pripyat, I'm from near Kiev.' Anastasia at once went up to the woman and asked what the matter was and why she'd mentioned Pripyat.

'Those radishes of hers are contaminated. She's brought the radiation with her ... Going round selling poisoned stuff – robbers,' said an angry old woman with a bunch of radishes.

'Ee, who knows eh? Where's the radiation from then? We're a canny way from Chernobyl – other side of Kiev! They didn't check us at home!'

'Guess what's going on in Kiev itself then? What're they selling in the markets there?' the woman waxed indignant.

A policeman arrived on the scene.

'Now then, Missus, clear your baskets out of here and don't let me catch sight of you here again. You people, don't form crowds, no crowding. That's not on. You've bought what you want, now go to your homes. Don't start a panic here. That's not on. This isn't Kiev.'

Advancing on some and pushing others, the policeman had dispersed the curious in a twinkling. Anastasia alone remained; he did not touch her.

'Please tell me what actually happened? I'm not a local. I'm from Leningrad Province.'

'Ah, that's why you're asking. You've not heard yet, I

dare say. Here in Moscow they're checking all the market produce. For radiation.'

'Do they find any?'

'Oh yes, all you want. You saw it yourself, just now.'

'What happens then?'

'We don't allow them to trade. What else can we do?'

'Is the contaminated stuff destroyed then?'

'No, no, where could we do it? We've got no orders to do that. Anyway these traders would just take advantage and claim compensation from us for destroying their property.'

'But in that case they could just take it to another market.'

'That's what they do. They go from market to market if they can nip inside, that is. If not, they sell the stuff outside the market round the corner. Folk buy if it's cheap enough. Anyway hell knows, this radiation ... you tell me what it is! Profiteers now ... what a swinish lot they are, I wish they could put an end to the lot of them and quick. And where are you from if you don't know the first thing?' The policeman recollected himself. 'Where are you from, Missus, eh? Got your little document? Passport?'

Anastasia meekly handed over her internal passport.

'Right. Svir, is it? What might your profession be?'

'Village headmistress.'

'Ah, well you're allowed to travel to Moscow. Take your little pass.'

Anastasia was about to enquire who wasn't allowed into Moscow and why, but felt shy of doing so. This policeman had enlightened her enough as it was. She changed her bag over to the other hand and set off quickly to give Natasha's children their treat. At home, however, she rinsed each berry for a long time under the tap. The radishes she had stuffed in a rubbish bin on the way.

Anastasia spent several days with Natasha and every day brought news of one sort or another about Chernobyl. A little information began to appear in the newspapers though more and more this tended to concentrate on the heroism of those who were working to counter the effects of the accident. As to the fate of the injured and the area's inhabitants in general, news was extremely sparse and bore all the signs of a cover-up.

All sorts of new people turned up at the house expressing interest in how things were going and from time to time bringing snippets of information. On one occasion someone brought along an American, an assistant to Professor Robert Gale, the bone-marrow specialist now working in Guskova's clinic. The American was clearly on his guard and gave away very little about the Chernobyl people; on the other hand he was eloquent about the dangers of nuclear war. The dissidents listened politely and gave Anastasia the opportunity to put questions, to which she responded with alacrity.

'Surely you must understand that my interest at the moment isn't in the supposed horrors of a third world war; what I'm worried about is the condition of people irradiated now, in peace-time. You don't have to propagandize me about peace and disarmament. I'm a communist myself, a headmistress and I hear these fine principles of yours every week in political studies at school, spoken by komsomols and pioneers. I'm interested in why you were invited to Moscow, what's happening to these irradiated people and the others.'

The American smiled to cover his embarrassment and suddenly spoke in quite a different tone.

'Why do you think I was invited to Moscow? Me, Doctor Gale, the other doctors and Armand Hammer that great friend of your country? For us it's a purely scientific visit, but not for your government, don't be deluded. Our Soviet colleagues could cope perfectly well without us; in this area they're on our level all right, they're as ignorant as we are. In all honesty, I'm not at all sure that bone-marrow transplants are needed at all with this sort of radiation damage. If a Soviet communist teacher can talk straight, I can give a straight answer. In my opinion our visit here has political motives. Your government has caused this disaster and now wants to present it as a common catastrophe for all humanity. That way they're relieved of the responsibility. The mysteries of the atom, unknown territory and all that ... That's why they let us come, it's an alibi for them. We don't know much either. Are the three hundred from

69

Chernobyl here in Moscow – how many in Kiev? We're not told. All I can say is that medical staff should keep all those who got severe doses of radiation in the first days of the accident under observation for a good many years. There are around a hundred thousand of those by our figures. There's nothing more I can tell you.'

Each evening Anastasia and Natasha spent hours by the radio, listening to Western stations. The news was guarded but it could be sensed that the speakers had much more alarming information than they felt able to impart to Soviet listeners, who had next to none. What made Anastasia marvel was the way Western citizens were recommended to behave with regard to increased radiation levels, what to avoid and what to use in the way of food. Natasha taped the advice of Western doctors and afterwards she and Anastasia sat till morning trying to sort out several copies, taking it in turn. Natasha's ancient Olympia could do only four copies, but in a night they did ten masters and so forty in all. 'If only Anna could see me now!' Anastasia thought to herself as she sat in her headphones in front of the tape-recorder and typewriter. 'Doesn't this make me a dissident?' But she was doing it only because it was something practical and necessary for a lot of people. She wouldn't have typed any political proclamations of course. 'Everybody has the right to information concerning their health. There's no politics in that,' she told herself.

At length she was told that a meeting with one of the sick Chernobyl people looked like coming off at Guskova's clinic. Natasha's friends undertook the arrangements. One of their grandmothers worked as a nurse in the Chernobyl section. It was she who took pity on the 'poor little teacher' looking for her sister and passed a message telling her to come on Sunday night when she was on duty and she would be taken round and introduced to 'her patients'.

It was after midnight when one of her new acquaintances drove Anastasia to Hospital No 6. By devious corridors he conducted her to the section yard where they had a good half-hour's wait by the hospital rubbish-bins. Finally the nurse emerged from what looked like a cellar-door carrying two pails.

'Oh dear, have you been here long? Well now, come with me. Here's a gown, put it on here. If anybody stops you, talk in some foreign language – they'll be too shy to ask you any questions, I expect. And you stay here young man, just here by the fence. Get down in the shadow of the bushes and wait till we come back.'

Anastasia shrouded herself in her white gown and followed the old woman.

The meeting took place in the section duty office. Anastasia was taken there by way of the administration quarters and the kitchen: the radiation sufferers were protected day and night from contact with visitors.

Anastasia sat for an appreciable time on a sofa and waited, agitatedly rehearsing the questions she would put to the invalid.

At last the door opened; he came in and sat down in an armchair. For a full minute Anastasia was unable to start the conversation: from the first sight of him she realized that before her was an incurable, terminally ill person and that his term of sickness had not long to run. He was not simply pale, there were no tints in his face at all. Sparse tufts of hair were slicked down to his head with grease of some sort. He had gone bald in patches – not with age. The most striking sign of illness was in his eyes. Remoteness and transparent anguish registered in them. He spoke first –

'You wanted to find out something about your relatives. Who are they?'

His voice was muffled and rustling as if he was speaking from behind a thick curtain.

Anastasia sighed and began.

'I'm looking for my sister, her children and her husband. This is the second week with no news. Her husband worked at the station, he's called Ivan Prikhotko. Do you know him by any chance?'

'Yes. And not by chance. We were workmates and friends. A good lad. He was lucky to have a wife like that, pure gold. Everybody loved Alenushka. Yes, and she was expecting a baby, poor thing!'

'She never wrote to me about that. Good God.'

71

'Too early to write, nothing to see. Ivan told me as a pal, a secret. Keep looking and looking for that sister of yours ... And I don't know anything about mine either. Alive are they, taken away somewhere? Don't worry, they say, they were all evacuated. If they were, why don't they write? If I only knew everything was all right ...'

Anastasia felt chilled: so that's how it was. Even people dying in this clinic, who got heroic odes written about them in the papers, even they couldn't find out where their relations were.

The sick man was sunk in his own thoughts and seemed to have forgotten about Anastasia.

'Please listen – so where was Ivan actually on that night?'

'Ivan? Ivan was on duty at the station that night.'

'And where is he now, do you know that?'

'Yes, he's in Mitino, a village. That's where they take our people.'

'You mean there's a special hospital there of some kind?'

'There's a special cemetery there. We all go there one by one. Ivan just finished his suffering sooner than the rest.'

Anastasia began to cry and wept for a long time. The Chernobyl man waited, calm and detached, till she got hold of herself. Or perhaps he'd forgotten her again ... finally Anastasia raised her head.

'Do you know anything else, about Alenushka?'

'No, I don't know anything about Alenushka. Maybe she was one of the wives near the station. They ran over there when they saw the glow from the fire and heard the ambulances on their way to the station. Of course they didn't let them into the grounds.

'So look for her in the evacuation somewhere. She might be still alive. Except they took all those wives away in the ambulances as well. They didn't let them go home.'

'Forgive me please for tormenting you with questions. I can see your mind's not on this. Just give me a suggestion, where can I find, or look for my sister?'

'If I only knew ... I'd have found my wife and kids. I just don't know whether she's scared of my illness and keeping away or whether she ... should I curse her or cry, I just

72

don't know. You go on to Kiev, it's nearer and you might find out. And listen, write down my wife and children's names and so on. I've begged and begged them here but they won't say a word. You might come across them on your travels. Tell them about me ... tell her to write, at least I'd know I'm going alone and haven't killed her and the kids as well. Write it down.'

'Of course I will. I promise wherever I look for mine, I'll keep an eye out for yours. Thank you for coming out here to see me, thank you. I hope you...'

'Don't bother,' the invalid interrupted. 'If you find my family, I'll pray for you over there. If God accepts Chernobyl people of course ...'

'Why, what do you mean?' whispered Anastasia, astonished.

'Don't you listen, I'm just talking. They're my other ideas. You wouldn't understand. If I'd had ideas like that earlier, Chernobyl wouldn't have happened. Well, goodbye now. I'm tired.'

He got up slowly from the chair and made his way to the door, slowly opened it and went out, without looking back at Anastasia. The white door closed soundlessly behind him.

On 11 May, 2827 inspections of incoming produce were carried out. All were free of contamination; 12 May 3501 tests revealed two contaminated; 13 May one out of 4621; 14 May seven out of 2726; 15 May six out of 3123; 16 May three out of 2920; 17 May one out of 3071; 18 May none out 3001; 19 May none out of 3017; 20 May one out of 3008.

Literary Gazette, 28 May 1986

It is important for the Chernobyl atom people to know that their families are safe and settled in ... But not all have had news yet from their families. It's no easy matter to establish contact immediately, after all, tens of thousands of people now have new addresses.

Trud, 7 May 1986

The wife of Leonid Telyatnikov, Lorisa Ivanovna and the children are now in Kiev. He says he has sent them two letters already, but has had no reply. He doesn't know how they are.

Izvestiya, 10 May 1986

I've got a wife and two children in Pripyat. Of course I'm worried. I know they're getting help, but where are they, how are they living, are they well?

D. Perch, Foreman,
electrical workshops, Chernobyl NPS
Socialist Industry, 8 May 1986

Initially we stored the clothing belonging to people coming in for treatment or investigation. In many cases these things are perfectly harmless after two weeks. Incidentally a special cleaning unit has been set up and anybody can have their clothing put to rights.

O. Schepin, USSR Deputy Health Minister
Literary Gazette, 21 May 1986

We're not covering anything up ... we publish our information openly and share it with foreign specialists.

Professor Angelina Guskova
APN, 14 May 1986

CHAPTER 8

Anna says goodbye to her Swedish friends

On the last day of Anna's stay in Sweden, Sven arranged a farewell supper at his hunting-lodge near Stockholm. Anna was in no mood for festivities but all the guests had been invited in advance, Faina well to the fore in this, and Anna could not bring herself to offend her by declining the unwanted celebration.

It was a candle-lit supper with Sven roasting game-birds from the cold-store. The hunting-lodge was in fact Sven's parents' old house, but they, along with Sven's brothers and sisters, had long ago moved to Stockholm and forgotten their peasant origins. They had wanted to sell the house, but Sven had begged it for himself, calling it his 'huntsman's hut'. The great kitchen with its hearth, he had converted into a hall. His guns adorned the walls, along with fishing gear and hunting trophies. The hall also contained an enormous pine table, knocked together by its owner. Skins of all kinds hung or lay about everywhere. Two of Sven's hunting dogs gave the 'hut' a special cosy feel and reminded Anna of life long ago in Svir: she and her sisters had owned two huskies, Enka and Dozor, one black and one ginger. Anna gave half an ear to Sven and Faina's conversation with their guests, Stockholm journalists and writers for the most part. She herself smiled absently and now and again put in a word or two by way of Sven, but her thoughts, or rather her feelings, were far away. She stroked the dogs, smelling the scent of the burning logs on the hearth and staring fixedly at the blaze: it all brought back poignant memories of other winter evenings when Anastasia would push her pile of marked exercise-books to one side and ask her sisters:

'Now then, all work done? What about a bit of twilighting, girls?'

They had no skins or fireplace; there was an old moth-eaten carpet, brought from the Leningrad flat, and a stove. They would spread the carpet out in front of the stove, open the lid and sit, all three of them, gazing at the flaring coals. It was the time when they could talk to one another about the things that mattered most, share their secrets or just sit in silence. It was nice being all three together in the warm, and the dogs as now lay alongside, staring into the fire ...

Anna had no wish to make a parade of her sadness in front of her guests, but sooner or later the conversation was bound to get round to Chernobyl, and so it turned out.

'What do you think of our ecologists? Instead of talking about who's to blame for the increased radiation in Europe, they're demanding the closure of all their own atomic stations, as if the Soviet Union and its atomic monsters had nothing to do with it!'

The speaker was Carola, a writer and editor of a woman's magazine, not surprisingly far from left-wing in outlook. Hari, who worked for a solidly respectable newspaper, though the reverse of that himself, was quick to respond:

'Well if we're opposed to nuclear energy, why shouldn't we regard this as a warning to us all?'

'Your paper sees things rather differently, Hari,' observed Faina Borisovna tartly.

'That's not my fault, it's my misfortune,' Hari countered. 'I may have to stay within the paper's position professionally, but I've never made any secret of my personal attitude.'

'What, you'd like to close all atomic power-stations?' asked Disa, who regarded herself as knowledgeable about the Soviet Union and life over there.

'Yes. The lot. At least for the moment, if disasters like Chernobyl are possible. The world's not ready to exploit atomic energy and Chernobyl's underlined the fact.'

'You don't think it's a purely Soviet problem?' asked Sven.

'No, I don't. It could happen in any country. What do you think, Anna?'

'I don't think it's a specifically Soviet problem. Especially as regards construction and safety. For me though the main point is different; up to now I've been unable to find out anything about what's happened to my relatives living in Chernobyl. What's more, nobody in the world knows exactly what the disaster was or the numbers of people affected. Now that's a purely Soviet problem, only the Soviets are to blame for that.'

'Yes, and it's very disappointing from the point of view of people who only wish the Soviet Union well,' Disa added. 'My friends and I believed that the new leadership in your country, Anna, would behave in a more democratic fashion. I think you'd agree that there were reasons for expecting something quite different from Gorbachev over Chernobyl.'

Anna smiled.

'I make it a point never to disagree with anyone in the West. I can only talk about our experience and express my own views. Well then, I think that one might have expected changes and that there have been and will continue to be such changes.'

'What, Annushka? You can't be serious.' Faina Borisovna roused herself to action.

'I'm saying what I think, like I always do. You know, don't you, Faina Borisovna, that industrial productivity has gone up considerably under Gorbachev?'

'Yes, that's a fact, but what's that got to do with it?'

'Just this, the fact shows how easy it was to raise that productivity. All it needed was a shout from upstairs. Somebody gets the sack, somebody else gets a warning and the old ramshackle machine gets going a bit faster. It can accelerate or slow down but it can't be renewed fundamentally. It's the same with democracy in our poor old country. We've got so much spare, such a backlog of inefficiency and lack of rights that it's easy for Gorbachev to look like a liberal reformer: he just has to tinker with this and that. There's enough slack for twenty or thirty years. For example, they've just gone and published the poems of Nikolai Gumilyov, who was shot during the 1920s. I'm sure even in my own country there's a lot of people clapping their hands and expecting better times just because of that.'

'But isn't that actually a sign of the democratization of society – and culture?'

'No, Disa, unfortunately not. While Gumilyov was not published, that was a real indication of the arbitrary power of the state in literature; the publication of his poetry now, despite the pluses, has one big minus which his suppression stood for. You can print the old suppressed poets at the rate of one a year and still retain an iron censorship over today's new young writers. You can let out ten thousand emigrés a year but that doesn't mean the frontiers are open. You could even release half the political detainees, but that doesn't mean freedom of speech for those who aren't even in camps. I'm glad about even the slightest relief in the existence of my people, even if it's only stopping the deliberate policy of making us a nation of drunkards, but I don't for one moment believe in Gorbachev the democrat.'

'But I've heard of one of your famous directors who's been invited to go back to the Soviet Union, and I think he's ready to do it. He believes he'll have total freedom in his work.'

'I think I can guess who you mean. I wish him luck, but I'll wait awhile before I pack my bags.'

'I understand what Anna's saying,' said Hari thoughtfully. 'Here's Gorbachev still keeping quiet over Chernobyl. He's been talking about anything you like to the West and his own people, but not about the thing that matters, the thing everybody's worried about. Yet, by all accounts, he must have known about the disaster the same day – with you it's the done thing to report whatever it is to the centre straight away isn't it, Anna?'

'Yes. I'm certain somebody high up at Chernobyl in the very first hour of the disaster was more worried about how he was going to report it "upstairs" so he could cover himself, than coping with what had happened.'

'So then,' Hari pursued, 'if Gorbachev had gone on television the same day, April 26th and honestly told what had happened to his people in the first instance and if a warning had come from Moscow to the West about having to take urgent measures, his authority would have gone up in everybody's eyes. What would you have said then, Anna?'

'I wouldn't have said anything. I'd have been packing my bags, or rather I'd have raced to the Soviet border without any bags, barefoot what's more!'

This brought applause from everyone, even Disa.

Then Carola spoke.

'You know I'm covering Chernobyl for our magazine, or rather Western assistance after Chernobyl. I've met a lot of businessmen in Sweden and Germany and French specialists in radiation sickness. What really surprised me was that a lot of Western institutions, firms and separate individuals offered help but they were refused. Sweden got an order to begin with for decontamination solution but later they didn't want it. Talks with a West German firm about the supply of robot-bulldozers were broken off unexpectedly. Also a well-known French radiologist said that Doctor Gale wasn't an expert in radiation diseases, though he certainly was in bone-marrow transplants. Besides, transplants of that sort are contra-indicated in the case of the Chernobyl people. What's the explanation of all that, Anna?'

'As regards methods of treatment, I can't say anything, I'm not a doctor. As for the rest I would suggest that politics is playing the main role here, that's the usual thing. Prestige comes into it: you know, we can cope with everything without any outside assistance – or observation. I smell a rat about this refusal of help as well. It's always been the same with us. In 1930 there was a terrible famine in the Ukraine and southern areas of the country and people were driven to cannibalism, eating corpses and their own children. The Soviet government took the sage decision to sell part of the harvest abroad, to stop people there "spreading rumours" about famine in the USSR.'

'Incidentally, the Soviet press is full these days of accusations of "gloating rumours about Chernobyl" in the West,' added Faina Borisovna.

'That's impossible!' cried Disa. 'How can there be any gloating here? Our paper was one of those which published that story about two thousand victims, but that was a rumour from Moscow, wasn't it?'

'As to that, let me tell you a Soviet joke. Is that all right? Well, listen. An American delegation comes to a collective farm by pure chance: the farm was a shabby affair but it had the same name, "Red Dawn", as an advanced farm in the next region where they always took foreigners. The chairman of the farm was away that day and the delegation was met by the office watchman, who conducted the Americans round the farm, the fields, everything. Next day, the chairman comes back and asks the watchman straight out: "They tell me, Arkhipich, it was you who took the Americans round the farm?" "I did." "Well, I hope you thought on to take them round the back ways, our central street's full of puddles and potholes you know." "Not I . . . I took them through the puddles." "What on earth did they have to say?" "They sounded surprised and they laughed." "Still, you didn't take them round the dairy? The roof's fallen in." "Not take them? Of course I took them! They gasped and laughed some more." "Well, at least you didn't show them the fields? They're all weeds." "I showed them the fields as well." "What did they do?" "Some sighed and some laughed." "Oh dear, Arkhipich, what on earth have you done? They'll describe all this in their papers!" "Never mind, let the sods slander us!"'

Faina Borisovna, when she'd had her laugh out, translated the story for the benefit of non-Russian speakers, acting the Russian characters beautifully. Taking advantage of the relaxed atmosphere, she at once suggested that the guests might like to stroll in the woods nearby, while Sven and Anna made tea and coffee for one and all.

Anna and Sven were left alone.

'Why've you been so sad all evening, Svenchik?'

'You haven't been too bright yourself.'

'I've got reason for that.'

'So have I.'

Anna didn't ask him for his reason, so Sven went on.

'You're going away, that's why.'

80

'Well, you knew my trip was nearly over. All lectures read.'

'But you've still got two weeks' holiday left. You could have stayed here.'

'Where's here?'

'I mean in this house, here. You like the place, I can see that. I'm right aren't I?'

'Yes you are, Sven, but I want to rest up a bit before the term starts. My eldest sister has decided to go on to Kiev to search for Alenka. She could need help at any moment. I'd like to gather my wits for a while and be ready for anything. I might have to do a lot of work, lecture outside the university, write articles for magazines.'

'Anna, if you don't want to stay here, then take me with you.'

'What a funny way of saying it: "take with with you", like a little boy.'

'It's your doing that I feel like a small boy next to you.'

'Do you like it?'

'If I'm honest, yes I do. You Russian women are so reliable, so strong.'

'D'you really know so many Russian women, Sven?'

'I know you and Faina and all those I've translated. Irina Ratushinskaya for example.'

'And you know as well, Sven, that even the strongest woman needs a man for defence, or support? There are times when you feel like just giving in and leaning on someone, maybe just for a minute or two, resting on someone's shoulder.'

'I know what you're getting at. You're right if you think I wouldn't be much support and protection in the life you led back home. I've no idea myself how I would behave in a situation like that. Living in your country, just to live and stay a simple ordinary person – that's something heroic. I'm not sure just how heroic I am. But we're in the West now, both of us, there are different yardsticks here and different worries and dangers. I just want to let you rest, guard you against life's problems. I can guess how hard it is for an emigré to adjust to living here and I want to stop you being so tired – and getting those shadows under the eyes in the evening.'

Sven cautiously drew the tips of his fingers along Anna's face, a timid caress which seemed to snap some hard, coiled spring inside her, causing her to sob and bury her face in his shoulder, or rather somewhere in his armpit, being on her level.

'Take me with you,' whispered Sven.

Chernobyl has become a test of the political morality of
the West.

APN, 19 May 1986

The worst thing is not the reactor accident in Block 4 of
the Chernobyl power-station, it is the rumours which
have fuelled the fantasies put about by our enemies.

Moscow Komsomolets, 22 May 1986

Through all the fuss over the accident at our nuclear
power-station hatred of the Soviet Union can be clearly
seen.

Georgi Arbatov
Moscow News, 18 May 1986

The real question lies in the deliberately inflated,
well-orchestrated fuss aimed at poisoning as far as
possible the atmosphere of East–West relations by a
miasma of anti-Soviet hysteria, cloaking a series of
criminally militaristic actions on the part of the USA and
NATO directed against the peace and safety of the
people of the world; the recent American aggression
against Libya, nuclear explosions in Nevada and the
militaristic 'star wars' programme.

Moscow News, 11 May 1986

I tell you honestly, my thoughts are anxious ones
today. Not because of the accident at the power-station
– progress is never easy. They're anxious because of
the tainted political atmosphere that Western circles
are trying to promote around this question.

Vladimir Gordon, war veteran from Moscow
Moscow Radio, 12 May 1986, 12–00

One Swedish firm offered us their services, via
intermediaries, in the area of anti-contaminant
chemicals. They wanted eighteen and a half dollars per

kilo. Today we have managed to put a similar liquid into production. The output is the same, thirty tons a day. The amount of foreign currency saved is easily calculated.

> Ivan Silayev, deputy chairman
> USSR Council of Ministers
> *Izvestiya*, 14 May 1986

'Olga Fyodorovna, what, in your opinion, was the main thing in M. S. Gorbachev's speech on television on May 14th?'
'I would say it was that he showed again how concerned the party is about ordinary Soviet people.'

> Olga Federenko, secondary school teacher,
> Ivankovsko region, Kiev Province
> *Radio Kiev*, 16 May, 9–00

There were no grounds for stirring up an agitation around the events at Chernobyl. It was done as a pretext to try and discredit the USSR and so weaken the effect of Soviet proposals for banning nuclear tests and abolishing nuclear weapons.

> Oleg Khlestov, USSR representative
> at the International Atomic
> Energy Agency (MAGATE)
> *APN*, 26 May 1986

CHAPTER 9
Anastasia flies to Kiev

The day after her meeting with the dying man from Chernobyl, Anastasia left by air for Kiev.

Her neighbour turned out to be an extremely garrulous middle-aged lady. After settling into her seat and fastening her belt in advance, the lady turned her attention to the passengers coming on board.

Catching sight of a young woman with two kiddies, she swivelled her considerable bulk towards Anastasia and demanded:

'Will you tell me why that crazy woman is taking her children? Is she fed up with them, or what?'

'Why shouldn't she fly to Kiev with her children?' asked Anastasia, astonished. 'Everything's supposed to be perfectly all right in Kiev.'

'Perfectly all right? If that was my flat-neighbour's idea of order I'd want to know why!'

'The papers say there's no danger at all for people living in Kiev.'

'The papers say! They write what they're told to write. You should listen to what the smart people say who ran away from "normal" Kiev without a backward glance.'

'What do they say?'

'They say that the hospitals are overflowing with radiation cases, that there's camps behind Chernobyl where they're going to keep everybody who got contaminated. Hold them, observe them and bury them. They say all Kiev's drinking contaminated water from the Dnepr, because there's nothing else. All their water's radioactive. They seem to be digging artesian wells in the middle of the town and laying piped supplies in from other rivers not affected. They also say that radioactive water has collected under Chernobyl and it's seeping underground. Wherever it goes, everything'll die there. Now you know where that madwoman is taking her lovely kids.'

'Well I think that's all rumours.'

'Rumours is it? Well listen to this then. Rumours are useful. If it wasn't for them, we'd never get to know anything except the Communist Party programme. It was Kievans themselves told me what went on there in the first days, the panic at the stations and the airport and how people just dropped everything they'd worked so hard for, grabbed the kids and a couple of suitcases and cleared out of the city. Can you imagine what the city authorities did? Forced people out to the Mayday demonstration! Straight into the radiation, poor things, column by column ... They say they took the irradiated people out of Chernobyl by the bus-load. Some of them to hospital and some straight to the cemetery, heaps and heaps of them in common graves.'

'How horrible! Did someone you know see that?'

'Nobody saw it. But plenty heard about it.'

During the flight, the voluble lady, with a glance round at their neighbours to ensure nobody was eavesdropping, edged closer to Anastasia and began talking in a whisper louder than the noise of the engines.

'You needn't believe the rumours, believe your papers if you like. I can see, can't I, a woman of the party before me?'

Anastasia nodded.

'Well then. I'm an observant person, life's taught me to pick out party people from a long way off. I'm a lot more afraid of party ladies than I am of men, but there's something about your face that inspires trust – there's something womanly in it, so I'm going to tell you what I saw with my own eyes in Moscow. My neighbour came in to me and asked me: "Viktoria Lvovna, would you like to come on a little trip out of town with me and my sister? I'll tell you straight away, our trip's not going to be very cheerful and it won't be like a picnic. My sister is going to her son's funeral, he died from radiation. She's already had one heart-attack and I'm very afraid something awful will happen to her at the funeral, it would be good if you were there. You're a strong, experienced sort of person!" Well if you want a decent life with your neighbours you have to give in to their least whim, so I went with them to the funeral. They took us about twenty kilometres out of Moscow in a kind of official black Volga, accompanied by a comrade. You know what I mean when I say "comrade". You don't talk much when one of them's around. So we didn't say a word the whole way. We got to Mitino village and there was a country churchyard there with a row of identical graves, about fifty. Some had stones, white marble, you know, but just names and dates. Where they'd lived and died – nothing else. Others were empty, waiting. So they let down my neighbour's nephew into one of those. The coffin was sealed and they wouldn't let the mother see her son. Next to us there were one or two more closed burials, and a comrade with them. We took the poor mother home all right and I asked my neighbour next day: "Anna Gavrilovna, what was all that, a strange funeral with no music, no flowers, no relatives? And why was it so far out of Moscow?" My neighbour says to me: "You just forget about all that, please, as if it never happened. My sister signed a form saying she'd keep quiet." Forms are forms but I guessed straight away where that poor boy was from we buried like a savage. And the same day I decided I had to fly straight to Kiev.'

'I'm sorry, but why?'

'I'm going there to save my child. My son Semochka works in Kiev, he's an electronics engineer. He's got a wife and two little girls. Semochka's a good father, he got to know about that disaster on 26 April and sent the girls to me in Moscow quick as a flash. Thank God they hadn't time in one day to be poisoned by the Kiev water. I found a private doctor on the side and he checked them for radiation. Both right as rain. Now I'm off there to fetch Semochka and his wife, Ira. I didn't send a telegram specially so he wouldn't come to meet me, though he has a car. No, I'll turn up in a taxi, ring the bell, walk in and say: "Pack straight away! Tomorrow you're flying to Moscow with me. We'll swap your flat for a Moscow one later." That's what I'll say to my son and his wife.'

'What if his bosses won't release your son from his work?'

'Bosses? Who could be more important than his mother, who brought him up and educated him without a father? They have their accidents and then decide if I can save my own children! You don't know my Semochka if you think his boss is more to him than his own mother's peace of mind. He'll do what his mother tells him, you'll see. I'm sorry, why are you going to Kiev then? You're not one of the bosses are you – there's a lot of them going there just now.'

'No. I'm going for about the same reason you are: I have to find my young sister and bring her out.'

'You're doing the right thing there. If they can't look after people, their families have to step in. Just don't let them give me those heroic fairy-tales about the whole country having to help Chernobyl. Those who haven't got other things to worry about can help the bosses, I'm going to help my relations. God won't ask me if I did voluntary overtime to help Chernobyl, he'll ask: "Viktoria Lvovna, where are your children, your grandchildren, is everything all right with them?"'

At this point, Anastasia's companion lost her breath in her excitement and glanced out of the window. Beyond the glass an enormous cumulus cloud was floating by, pierced by shafts of sunlight, like lightning. Viktoria Lvovna continued, addressing herself directly to this heavenly wanderer:

'And I'll say to God: "You know whether it was easy for me, Lord. I didn't keep my husband and buried my father and mother early as well. I was a helpless daughter and a timid wife. But you know, Lord, what torments I went through bringing up Semochka and teaching him. In school I argued with the teachers over every mark he got and Semochka got the gold medal. How many shoes did I wear out and how much money did I spend getting my boy into the institute? When he was ill I didn't get that drop-in doctor from the regional clinic, I got a private doctor, German Andreyevich and for every visit, Semochka's mam paid him twenty roubles out of her eighty-rouble salary. And when you, Lord, allowed that accident at Chernobyl, was I not to save him and his family, so they wouldn't drink that tainted water?"' Here Viktoria Lvovna addressed her remarks to Anastasia, not God, 'In three days there won't be hide or hair left of Semochka in Kiev. What do you think God will say to that?'

'I don't know.'

'I'll tell you, then. He'll say to me: "Viktoria Lvovna, you've done everything a mother should and I have no criticism of you." But those who let loose radiation on innocent children, what won't he have to say to them! There's no good coming to them, believe you me!'

At this point the stewardesses began handing out breakfast and the conversation was interrupted. After the meal, Viktoria took a large warm kerchief from her bag, wrapped it round her legs and dropped off to sleep, after counselling Anastasia to do the same. She, however, did not sleep, but continued to ponder her companion's words: how much truth could there really be in all these rumours she had been retailing? And what was going on – why were the country's leaders so afraid of giving people full and precise information? If people had had a complete picture of what had taken place in and around Chernobyl wouldn't it have been easier for them to get their bearings in the situation, wouldn't there have been less panic and fewer stupid rumours? No doubt Semochka hadn't been the only one to send his children to their grandmother, as far as possible out of Chernobyl. How did people get on who had no relatives in other towns? Had they gone off into the blue, clutching their children? How many had run away from danger? If the authorities clamped down on information, afraid of panic, their wisdom was open to question – the unknown is the mother of panic.

Anastasia spent the remainder of the flight in similar musings, until the aircraft landed at Borispolye aerodrome. Anastasia had no luggage apart from a travelling bag, but her neighbour requested her to carry her cases as far as the taxi. 'You have to give in to your neighbours' least whim,' Anastasia recalled Viktoria Lvovna's words, and smilingly agreed. The baggage hall was not too crowded but when they emerged into the main hall with Viktoria Lvovna's cases they were astonished to see immense queues at the ticket windows and people sitting in the aisles, on their luggage, anywhere they could find a space. Policemen scurried about the hall as well as some thuggish individuals in plain clothes. On their way to the exit, they overheard an unusual announcement: 'Passengers for the Moscow flight must pass through the medical check-point.'

'I wonder what that means?' said Anastasia.

'Can't you guess? They're checking them for radiation, that's what.'

They parted at the taxi rank.

Natasha had furnished Anastasia with the addresses of her friends in Kiev, but she also had one of her own, an old friend from her institute days. She set off for that one, resolving to save Natasha's list for emergencies. Back in Moscow, she had observed some suspicious-looking young men following her and that lay behind her decision not to get in touch with the Kiev dissidents unless really pressed.

The First of May, Kiev, October Revolution Square. 10 AM. The holiday demonstration is beginning. The loudspeakers broadcast the words of the Mayday Slogans of the Central Committee of the CPSU. A mighty wave, thousands strong, rolls back in reply, 'Hoorah.' ... We celebrate this Mayday in the midst of a general upsurge in the economy in response to the historic resolutions of the XXVII Party Congress. Our party has the wise eyes of Lenin ... The columns march, one giving way to the next, time and again the festive city gives out its many-voiced 'Hoorah.'

Pravda, Ukraine, 2 May 1986

It's natural that people in Kiev are following reports from Chernobyl power-station with particular interest – it's 150 kilometres from there.

Radio Mayak, 7 May 1986, 19–30

Indeed, at first Kievans did not have complete information on what was going on or the situation in the town. This spawned all kinds of rumours, which were, incidentally, avidly spread by sundry Western 'voices'.

Pravda, 9 May 1986

Openness is a pledge that measures to deal with the consequences of the accident, outlined and to some extent already implemented, will be interpreted correctly and carried out strictly.

Komsomolskaya Pravda, 13 May 1986

Here one should be aware of potential danger of another kind – a tendency towards alarming the people. That is why we are categorically opposed to such a tendency, termed in the language of some zealous accusers 'exhaustive information'.

Viktor Sidorenko, First Deputy Chairman, USSR State Control Committee for Atomic Energy Safety

APN, 26 May

91

The most widespread claims are now about the incompleteness of information. But let us be realistic: the government decision was taken literally within hours.

> Boris Scherbina, Deputy Chairman,
> USSR Council of Ministers, at a
> press conference at the USSR Ministry
> of Internal Affairs, 6 May 1986

Strict checks are being imposed on outward-bound travellers at airports, railway and bus terminals. The aim is to bring medical first-aid to those in need of it.

> V. Vetchinkin, Chief of
> Main Nursing Services, Ukraine
> *Izvestiya*, 9 May 1986

If you wish to have objective information about Soviet Ukraine, listen in to our 'Informational Programme' every evening at this time. Our motto: 'truthful and effective information'.

> *Radio Kiev*, 19 May 1986, 23–00

CHAPTER 10

Anastasia talks to her friends in Kiev

On the way from Borispolye into Kiev Anastasia noted the ceaseless flow of traffic on both sides of the road and the multitude of police posts: these stood at all cross-roads and exits. She couldn't bring herself to quiz the driver about the reason for this, recalling some remarks of Natasha's friends to the effect that the KGB did some recruiting among taxi-drivers. Still, she could easily understand that it was connected with Chernobyl and the peculiar conditions of life in Kiev Province.

As they were crossing Paton bridge, Anastasia saw with alarm the empty river below completely bare of craft and the great stretches of beach totally deserted. As the taxi left the bridge she saw close by on the bank a board with 'Bathing forbidden. Danger!' in large letters. She drew a sigh and began to wonder what awaited her in Kiev.

Before she left Moscow, Anastasia had phoned her friend Tatyana with whom she intended to stay for a few days. Naturally she was delighted to accommodate her, advising her only that as she worked in the mornings she couldn't come to meet the plane but would certainly be at home when Anastasia arrived.

At one time Tatyana had studied in the same faculty as Anastasia and now taught Russian to foreign students in Kiev. She and her husband, a well-known cardiologist there, used to stay in Anastasia's flat whenever they happened to be in Leningrad and Anastasia had spent a holiday with them some ten years previously.

Tatyana lived in the centre of the city on one of the side roads leading into the Kreschatik and while they drove, Anastasia tried to discern anything unusual in the way the city or its people looked.

The chestnuts were flowering, the same Kiev chestnuts which began every report from the city, even those that concerned the Chernobyl disaster. For some reason, journalists had concluded that news of the chestnuts flowering at the due time must have a reassuring effect.

What was unusual struck the eye at once: there were virtually no children in the streets. There were occasional groups of schoolchildren but no sign at all of toddlers. Once only, at a street crossing, did a young mother wheel a pram in front of the taxi, but the hood was raised and draped with white curtain material. The people were all wearing head-gear of some sort, sometimes too heavy for the hot weather. There was none of the usual springtime street-vendors' trays with ice-cream, pasties and fizzy drinks.

Tatyana hugged Anastasia and smothered her with kisses, but on looking her over, shook her head:

'You're cracking up, Nastenka, cracking up. Not the heart is it? Alexey had better have a listen to you. He's not at the clinic any more though: he got sick of struggling with the reactionaries over there, so he gave in and went to work at an epidemic emergency station. It's like going on pension for him. You'll see what a grumbling old thing he has turned into. You, of course, he'll check over.'

'No, no, Tanyusha, no need for anything like that. My heart *is* acting up quite a bit but I haven't time to worry about that now. Let's hope it'll hold out while it's needed. The main thing for me now is to find Alenka.'

'Still no news? Yes, there's a lot of families lost contact. Just like the war...but good for you that you've come. Alexey will be home from work in a minute and we'll put our heads together and think what we can do. Now into the kitchen, we'll have a chat over tea.'

Even in Tatyana's kitchen Anastasia noticed changes. On her previous visit it had been full of fruit and greens – they were both confirmed vegetarians. Now in place of the greens, fruit and berries, there were jars of preserves and bottles of fruit-juice on the table and shelves.

'You're not eating fresh fruit and vegetables at all?' asked Anastasia.

'We're taking no chances. We just buy what comes in from other republics at the market. They test all the stuff with dosimeters, but there are cases where bribery lets in contaminated things. So we eat only the imported stuff. And we wash them time and again: dust gets everywhere, and that's... well, you know yourself... And there's been no rain for ages, just to spite us, that would wash down the city properly. Alexey tells me to wash every berry separately under the tap, then rinse them in mineral water and dry them off with a towel. We're nearly washed away, we wash our hair every day, though I never go out bare-headed now.'

'Are things really as serious as that?'

'I'll show you if you like. Come out on to the balcony.'

Tatyana led Anastasia through the sitting-room; the balcony was swathed in muslin on all sides.

'This is Alexey's invention, and torture for me I can tell you, this muslin. I have to sprinkle it morning and after-noon – and wash it at night, in gloves, he's very strict about that. I'm not a medic and I'm not used to working in gloves. I keep slipping them off when he's not looking. So we only air the flat through the balcony window, all the other windows are sealed up tight. But that's not what I wanted to show you.'

Tatyana pulled out from her pocket a small instrument, rather like a fountain-pen, and brought it near the muslin. A faint crackling could be heard.

'A Geiger counter?'

'That's what it is. Alexey brought one back from work on the sly.'

She took the instrument away but the barely audible crackle persisted. She put it to Anastasia's hair and the rattle became louder.

'Hear that? And how many minutes were you outside?'

'Oh, about half an hour waiting for a taxi. That's not a lot of radiation, is it?'

'No, no. Not much. But a bit more than an hour, two,

three and it would amount to a nice little cancerkin as my Alexey puts it in his jolly way.'

They returned to the kitchen.

'Perhaps you'd prefer coffee to tea? You're looking really done-in, was it the journey?'

'Probably. Tell me, is it true the radiation victims aren't just in Moscow, and Kiev's chock-full of them as well? A woman on the plane filled me up with horror stories, my hair stood on end.'

'Yes, there's plenty of rumours going the rounds but there's enough horrors too. The official casualty numbers are far too low. They mainly talk about the ones who got to Moscow. How many have we got? In the province? White Russia's keeping quiet about its cases as well, and they've had some. There's a lot of sick doctors from Chernobyl and Pripyat, they're working up there without reliefs. One doctor gets irradiated and drops, that's the time they take him off to hospital and send another one in his place. It doesn't enter anybody's head to relieve the lot at once – who with, though? When Alexey gets back from work he can give you the details, what the medics are going through. Incidentally, there's a lot of women up there. No, they just don't give a damn about people!'

Closely as Anastasia was listening, she noticed that her friend filled the coffee-pot, not with tap water, but with 'Narzan' mineral water.

'What's this, a new-fangled way of doing coffee – mineral water?'

'That's just what it is, new-fangled. It's a real fight getting mineral water – Alexey categorically forbids me to use tap water for coffee.'

'Really? I read in the papers that the water in Kiev reservoir, and the Dnepr and the Pripyat was all all right.'

'If everything was all right, why are there so many announcements in the press about it? Are you a little girl, or what?'

'You mean things are a lot more serious than the papers say?'

'Of course they are. Children are recommended to stay indoors except in case of need. I can tell you in confidence that the evacuation of all children from Kiev was discussed. It should have been done from the start but they're in no hurry, thinking of the panicking parents. So they decided not to evacuate them, just shorten the academic year and send them on their holidays early. That'll look more dignified. Just remember all these are secrets I'm blabbing to you Anastasia, so don't give me away. My secondary school colleagues told me how they had to hide their blushes in front of the parents who ask them when they should take their holidays so they can take the kids further away. The teachers are told to lie and say that the exams and the holidays will be at the usual time. And tell them off for "spreading ridiculous rumours and sowing panic". The holidays are actually starting on May the 15th but they're only going to announce it a day or two in advance.'

'Why keep it back from the parents? They really won't be able to go on holiday with the children that way.'

'That's why they're doing it, darling. The children go away and the parents stay behind and fulfil the plan – in accordance with the resolutions of the XXVIIth Party Congress.'

Anastasia caught herself thinking that Tatyana's thrust at the party had not annoyed her in the least.

'See when they issued medical recommendations – day eleven! There, look, yesterday's paper – May the 6th. They're criminals because the half-life of radioactive iodine is eight days. Iodine 131, have you heard of that? Our institute has its swine as well.' Tatyana went on: 'The students from capitalist countries packed and went as soon as they heard about the accident. The poor fish from the developing countries who get their grant from us were forced by the management to call those who left panickers and Western slanderers. Even now they're exposing "accursed imperialist plots". Just listen to them at meetings saying they never felt better in their lives, breathing radioactive dust.'

'Have doctors had a look at them?'

'Why should they, they're not complaining.'

They had reached their third cup of coffee when Tatyana's husband came in from work. He and Anastasia

97

barely recognized each other, after only three years. Whether it was the professional difficulties which had forced Alexey to leave the clinic or something else had bowed him, he looked years older; his back was bent and his hair grey. On his face Anastasia read that she herself had not changed for the better.

Alexey pulled up a chair and Tatyana served dinner. Afterwards they moved to the sitting-room.

'What's new, Alyosha?' asked Tatyana.

'What could be new? Well, they're going to bore some more artesian wells.'

'Lord! How many of those things have they drilled in the last few days?'

'So far only at the really important installations: dairies, the meat combine and the other food factories. The city goes on drinking that filth. Aqueducts will have to be built to avoid the dangerous water sources.'

'What sort of aqueducts?'

'To a historian I can explain very simply. It's a modern aqueduct on the Roman model, built above ground.'

'Because it's cheaper that way?'

'That's it. Unlike the Roman structure this is temporary, they can take it down and use the pipes somewhere else.'

'But it can't be built all that quickly. A whole aqueduct above ground!'

'"A whole aqueduct" – wouldn't you like two? A second one's being planned at the moment!'

'Now you know why I make coffee with mineral water,' said Tatyana.

'Nastenka, what plans have you got in Kiev, how are you going about looking for Alenka?' Alexey asked her.

'Well, I thought I would try the Kiev Provincial Party Committee and the same at the Komsomol level. Alenka was still Komsomol age and should be in their records. I read in some paper as well that they took pregnant women and mothers with small children first and put them in a sanatorium. It seems Alenka was expecting her third child. Perhaps she's in that sanatorium with the kids?'

Alexey nodded.

'Good thinking. I have heard it said that the party

organizations aren't giving out information on relatives to anybody but they might do something in your case: you're a party member of long standing and you've come a long way. Above all, try and find out if your nephews are in the children's hospital, where they took those who'd got a dose.'

'What? There aren't child casualties are there?'

'Nastenka, you're an intelligent person. Just think, how could there not be if the accident took place on a Friday night and children were sent to school in Chernobyl and Pripyat as if nothing had happened on Saturday morning? The little ones of course didn't go to the creches and kindergartens but their mothers took them outside, it being a Saturday. It doesn't take much to irradiate a toddler. On the Sunday, the evacuation didn't get under way till two in the afternoon, so the kids were out till lunchtime. The weather was beautiful and not many knew about the radiation.'

Anastasia's thoughts were grim.

'I'm sorry now I didn't go to Ivan's grave when I was in Moscow.'

'You know where he's buried?'

'Yes, in Mitino, along with the others from Chernobyl who had already died in Moscow. If I find Alenka what will I tell her?'

'She's got to be found first,' sighed Tatyana.

'How did you come to find out where he's buried?'

'I talked with a friend of his from the power-station.'

'In Guskova's clinic?'

'Yes.'

'I really want to ask you, Nastenka, how you managed to get in there and fix a meeting?'

'What? You got permission for a meeting?' asked Tatyana, astonished.

'No permission, I wormed my way in. Illegally of course!'

Alexey smiled and shook his head.

'So, Nastenka, you're not so "correct" as we all used to think you. You sit there and all the time inside you there's a simple Russian woman ready to "rush into a blazing hut".'

'A good woman rushes in and comes out again, Alyosha,' Tatyana added. 'So let's give her a hand to get in every door and come back out again. Otherwise it'll be the same story we had with Yerofeyev.'

'What Yerofeyev's this?' enquired Anastasia.

'One of our teachers. His son had gone over to Pripyat when it happened. An engineer, nothing to do with the station, a radio engineer. There's a radio factory over there. Well, he didn't come back so the father rushed over to the Provincial Committee and started demanding that they help him to find his son. Then he went missing himself. The son came back after two days and now he's looking for his father round all the mental hospitals. So we're not going to let Alenka go off campaigning on her own. You're on the evening shift tomorrow aren't you? Well you could go with her to the Provincial Health Department in the morning, then do the round of the hospitals. I'll do a couple of lectures in the morning and get off work for the afternoon. After lunch, you and I, Nastenka, will pay a visit to the party and the Komsomol. We're not letting you go anywhere on your own, isn't that right, Alyosha?'

'Of course it is! Tatyana's talking sense, it happens with her at times. If your tongue got you as far as Kiev that's no guarantee it won't get you a bit further than you want – where Makar never drove his cows. Are we agreed?'

'Agreed. Thank you both, my dears.'

'Never mind that, you can say your thank-yous when we've found Alenka. Well, how's your other sister, Anna? Hasn't she got married to some lord over there?'

'Well no, it seems. She's lecturing in Sweden at the moment. She's very worried about Alenka as well. It was she who first told me there'd been an accident at Chernobyl, while they were still keeping quiet on the subject here.'

'So then, you didn't reject your sister over your party card? You're still keeping in contact – good for you! Tatyana's told you I left the job?'

'No, I didn't have time. I just said you worked at an epidemic emergency station. You tell her, it'll be interesting for her and take her mind off things.'

'True enough. Nothing makes us feel better than to hear

tell of someone else's troubles. It happened like this. I had this old friend, wonderful doctor and a wonderful man, too. We both did heart surgery and wrote several bits of work together. Two years ago he left for Israel, got fixed up marvellously and started ringing me at the clinic. As you might think, we talked about professional matters now and again. That's where our vigilant mediocrities caught me out. They're the ones who progress slowly in medicine but pretty quick up the party-admin ladder. They reported that I was supposed to be giving away Soviet medical secrets to my former colleague. So they started putting pressure on me. Reports, questioning. Eventually I got summoned to the place you know of where I was ordered to cease my telephone-calls and correspondence with my friend. I for my part told them where they could go, politely of course. So I had to leave my job. Just as well doctors are in short supply, you can always get fixed up.'

Anastasia listened to Alexey's tale, without saying a word about not ringing or writing to Anna herself for seven years. It wasn't that she was ashamed, though she was; she just didn't have the strength to explain it all and justify herself. Not up to it.

They went to bed early. Alexey reminded Anastasia to take a shower before turning in and wash her hair thoroughly as well.

'Alyosha! I've only been in the open air half an hour!'

'Never mind. Orders is orders, you'll wash it every day even if you've never left the house. Anyway in these matters I demand total obedience and discipline. Is my requalification from cardiologist to health adviser to be in vain?'

Radiation levels in Kiev do not exceed the levels of solar radiation in the southern Crimea resorts in July.

Ukraine SSR Minister of Health,
Anatoli Romanenko
Kiev television, 8 May 1986

In May, Kiev is always unique. The chestnuts blossom, the gardens are ablaze with their snow-white crowns...

Pravda, 9 May 1986

The first thing to strike the eye is the normality of life in Kiev. Mothers wheel prams along the streets, the world cycling championships were in full swing.

Soviet Russia, 13 May 1986

According to our calculations the background radiation in Kiev should return to normal somewhere around 19 May.

Professor M. Shandala
Izvestiya, 12 May 1986

The Republic Ministry of Health considers it appropriate to bring to the attention of residents in Kiev and Kiev Province recommendations, compliance with which will assist in reducing the possible effect of radioactive substances on citizens.*

Kiev Radio, 6 May 1986, 06–00

Schools in Kiev present an unusual sight at the present time. You will not see the normal crowds of children in the yards and on the playing-fields. Teachers are making sure that children do not leave the buildings.

Head of Kiev Education Administration – A. Tymchuk
Izvestiya, 9 May 1986

I get angry when certain people in the city put about silly rumours. The schools are supposed to be closing and children sent out of the city. Because of this some people go about with long faces and a mood of depression.

---

*Ten days after the Chernobyl accident (J.V.)

I know that the school exams start on 25 May. Why spread rumours like this?! Just write this: health worker Kuzmenko knows for a fact, not via rumours, that there is no danger to people's health in Kiev!

Pravda, 9 May 1986

In Kiev, the academic year for years 1–7 will end on 15 May. Children in those classes will be sent to summer holiday camps and health establishments in other provinces in the republic.

Izvestiya, 13 May 1986

The streets of Kiev are as crowded with young people as ever, but if you look more closely, you will notice very few kids in the city.

Literary Gazette, 4 June 1986

From today virtually all schoolchildren from those regions of Kiev Province which accepted evacuees from the Chernobyl accident zone are being sent to pioneer camps. Next to go will be junior classes from Kiev. Although medical workers have passed the children as healthy, in present circumstances it is considered desirable to provide them with an extended recreation period. The holidays, including travel to camps on the Black Sea, are free.

Radio Mayak, 14 May 1986, 18–00

Neither the Dnepr, along its entire length, nor, of course, the Black Sea, received any radioactive influx.

Yuri Israel,
Chairman of USSR Committee for
Hydrometeorology and Control of the
Environment
APN, 12 May 1986

The Kiev reservoir is the basic drinking 'cup' of the city. Control posts were set up immediately following the accident, along its entire length as well as on the River Pripyat.

The results of their analyses, taken every hour, confirm that there is no danger of any kind.

Chairman Ukraine Council of Ministers,
A Lyashko
Izvestiya, 10 May 1986

A package of measures has been worked out, providing for, in particular, a wider utilization of water from the River Desna together with artesian wells.

Chief Health Officer Ukraine,
Anatoli Kasyanenko
Pravda Ukraine, 10 May 1986

Through the timely implementation of the proposed measures, the inhabitants of Kiev and other towns on the Dnepr will be guaranteed pure drinking water. Our chemists in a very short period of time have devised methods of filtration and cleansing drinking water from the Dnepr.

President of Ukrainian Academy of Sciences,
Boris Paton
Moscow News, 22 June 1986

As is well-known, after the nuclear power-station accident, all produce, including market produce, goes through dosimeter monitoring. Some traders try to evade the new trading-laws by using bribery.

Radyanska Ukraina, 18 June 1986

Eight thousand foreign students are enrolled in Kiev higher education institutes. Only eight of these have left the city.

Izvestiya, 13 May 1986

As is well-known, out of more than eight thousand foreign students, only 250 have left.

Pravda Ukraine, 28 May 1986

CHAPTER 11

Anna and Sven on holiday in the Alps

Anna and Sven reached the Alps from Stockholm in a day and a half, staying overnight in Frankfurt-am-Main with the Belovs, friends of Anna. It was the first time in seven years that Anna had driven such a long way in a car and she found to her surprise that it was by no means as tiring as she had imagined. Seeing Anna's enthusiasm, Sven suggested sweeping past the Alps into Italy, and finally Venice, but Anna wouldn't agree. It was important for her to have a telephone at hand and a permanent number. She had been out of contact with Anastasia for three days and she couldn't wait to stop somewhere. They reached Garmisch but there were too many people there. They turned left and drove along the Austrian frontier, straying now into Austria then returning to Germany: the border was serpentine at this point. Sven remained unmoved by these excursions but Anna derived a genuine pleasure from them.

'Another fifteen minutes' drive in Austria with no visa and no hassle!'

'What's so amazing about that?' Sven was puzzled.

'Well, if you see the Soviet frontier any time, if only from socialist Poland, then you'll understand. Every kilometre's got enough barbed wire for three concentration camps.'

'It must be awful to live knowing you're behind barbed wire, if the whole country's fenced off.'

'When you realize, it is awful. That's why people emigrate. Look Svenchik, Austria again!'

105

On the verge appeared a frontier post with a board bearing the sign Republic of Austria; Anna laughed joyously. Sven glanced sideways at her, smiling.

'You know Anna, it's only when I'm with you that I realize how free people are here. I can only sense the joy of it through you.'

'I should think so! It's easy enough to understand, you can't get emotional over what you breathe like air. I remind you that freedom is both a miracle and a natural right – isn't that it? But there is one thing even more important for us Russians than freedom. Liberty. But that I *can't* explain to you.'

'Is there really any difference between "freedom" and "liberty"?'

'There's a very big one: liberty is greater than freedom. Without freedom it's nauseating, but without liberty, it's stifling. I just drink in the freedom here, but I have very little in the way of liberty.'

Sven again glanced at her.

'Anarchy?'

'Not at all! But I don't know how to explain it to you. In the camp where there wasn't a trace of freedom I had free will, you see.'

'Internal freedom?'

'That's getting warm. But it isn't quite that either. Anyway no explanations now – later when I've got some Russian books handy, OK?'

Sven, of course, agreed to wait, overjoyed that Anna was taking it as a matter of course that they would be together in the future somewhere where there would be lots of Russian books.

While talking they had not been neglecting to keep an eye out on both sides for a place to spend the night. They passed through mountain villages and little towns but every time Anna said:

'This one's not right. I want everything to be together: stream, lake, forest and mountains. And no fuss.'

Suddenly they saw a turn-off with a sign: 'Private Road'.

'Oh, a private road. Does that mean you can't drive

106

along it? What do you think, Sven? The road's so pretty as well, going along by the river.'

'I don't think so,' said Sven. 'Probably you just have to pay a toll here.'

So it turned out. A wooden toll-booth manned by a genial fat Bavarian stood by the roadside. He calmly suggested they pay four marks and told them that ahead lay houses and villages where one could get a room, and large lakes with hotels on the shore.

They drove on along the private road which wound along by a fast-flowing mountain stream. On the other side towered snow-capped mountain summits. The stream itself was extremely picturesque, dividing round green islands and pebbly shoals before flowing together once more. There were very few cars on the road, only three or four coming towards them and none, it seemed, on their side of the road.

'It looks like there are places here wild enough for you Anna, what do you think?'

'Could be. As long as my Germans only avoid it for economic reasons. The Russian emigrés tease them for being crazy over economizing.'

'They wouldn't have such a rich country if they hadn't known how to economize.'

'And work, Sven. That matters more.'

'Well you, as I understand it, don't know how to economize at all.'

'Does that annoy you?'

'Not a bit. Just the opposite, I'm glad.'

Actually, Sven was pleased because Anna had phrased her question implying that an affirmative answer would have annoyed her. Sven still had no idea whether Anna was really prepared to link her future with him; she gave evasive replies to any direct question and quickly changed the subject. So, as a result, he tried to guess at her mood by way of various oblique indications.

Soon they came out on to the shore of a huge lake. The view was magnificent but at once Anna announced decisively:

'We'll come back here, but we'll put up somewhere

else. See, there's a hotel there, and another, it's not for us.'

The house they chose was spotted by Anna as soon as it came into view round a bend. A large, lonely house with the usual wooden verandah running round it, hung about with geraniums.

'Just look how sweet it is, Sven. The one and only house on the entire mountain and no sign of a village anywhere near. And a cowshed and cows grazing in the meadow. I think we've arrived. Let's hope they have rooms!'

There was one free room in the house, not expensive and extremely comfortable: it was a corner room with a way out on to the verandah. After a second's thought, as it seemed to Sven, Anna said that the room would suit them. The landlady, a splendid-looking lady of about forty, made them welcome and helped them with their luggage from the car, informing them that up ahead was a small settlement with a restaurant where they could have dinner. Breakfast was included in the thirty marks for the room.

Anna at once enquired whether she could use the telephone, and the landlady conducted her into a lower hall, told her the number of the hotel and indicated the phone. Anna immediately rang Faina Borisovna and asked her to take the phone number of the hotel in case Anastasia rang from Kiev.

After that she and Sven showered in turn and walked to the restaurant for dinner. They chose the furthest table, which had a low wooden screen separating it from the rest of the hall. A waitress in Bavarian costume, with plaits made up basket fashion, brought the menu.

'Look Sven, all that game and venison.'

'Mm, do you like game?'

'Adore it!'

'You'd make a good wife for a hunter.'

Anna nodded, continuing her deep study of the menu. Once again Sven tried to fathom whether her nod meant anything concrete.

They ordered venison schnitzel and Sven chose the

wine. While the meal was in progress, Anna did not fail to look about her, at the same time insisting that Sven notice the ancient fireplace in the corner, the cuckoo-clock, the Bavarian waitresses' hair-styles. Sven had never suspected her capacity to draw pleasure from such trifles and he was excited to observe the changes taking place in Anna during their short trip. He had expected changes: when she had so decisively agreed to his accompanying her to Germany he saw that some sort of barrier had been overcome inside her. But Sven had thought that Anna, always so calm and restrained, would wake to womanhood. Instead the girl in her had woken, almost a child – that Sven had not bargained for. It even frightened him. It had been odd seeing this childish glee and hearing the continual 'Look, Sven'. This was an Anna he had not known.

A crowd of young Germans arrived and took the next table. The waitress placed a huge mug of beer in front of each and the newcomers started a discussion. Anna lent an ear to this and frowned.

'What are they on about?' asked Sven, whose knowledge of German was less than Anna's 'on the gastronomic level', as he confessed.

'Nuclear power-stations. They're arguing about whether they're necessary or not.'

'And what do they think?'

'They're all against, they're just arguing about whether "alternative" forms of energy are enough ... now they're listing all the accidents they've heard of in various countries. They're ordinary folk and they've got the normal attitudes about it: if it's dangerous to people, that means it's premature, economics and finance don't bother them much. Still, Sven, let's move to another table. Otherwise we'll get drawn in and start our own discussion.'

The waitress was surprised but made no objection to their moving to another corner.

In their new places, Anna drew a hand across her forehead and adjusted her hair.

'I won't. I don't want to think about it today. Let's have one evening without that.'

Sven stroked her hand and his questioning eye fell on a large boar's head on the wall.

'You know, I've never yet hunted a wild boar. I'll have to give it a try.'

'Of course, you're more a lion man, aren't you?'

'You can't needle me. I have actually hunted lions, not with a rifle though, a camera. I was on a safari in Africa.'

'Oho, let's have the story.'

Sven began his tale, noting the shadow caused by the overheard conversation slowing quitting Anna's face. After that, she told Sven how she had gone with local hunters in Svir, in pursuit of an elk. Then, carried away, she began describing the forest at Svir, where she had lived with Anastasia and Alenka...

By dessert Anna's gaiety suddenly disappeared and she fell silent.

'Tired?' asked Sven, taking her hand. Anna quietly released her hand and made no reply. Nevertheless a minute later she announced that she now wanted ice-cream. It was brought, but when Sven had finished his, Anna was still toying with her first spoonful. Sven realized now that she was simply spinning out time so as not to go home; she was afraid of being along with him and feared the intimacy that it would bring. Recognizing the situation, Sven was immediately aware of a surge of virility. For the first time since they had known each other he saw that the initiative had passed to him. He resolved not to let slip the opportunity.

'Time to go, Anna,' he said and summoned the waitress.

Back in their room, Anna at once opened her suitcase and set about hanging up her dresses in the wardrobe and sorting out her things. He, meanwhile, seated himself in an easy chair, folded his arms and fixed his eyes unblinkingly upon her. Anna felt his gaze, but pretended to be wholly engrossed in her unpacking, even humming a tune to indicate total absorption in her activity. Her voice trembled slightly during the performance, however.

'Come here Anna,' Sven summoned her quietly.

'I can't Sven,' she replied petulantly, sinking to her

knees before the case and burying her face in a sweater. 'You can see I have to sort everything out, I packed it any old how and I can't find a thing.'

At this, Sven rose from his chair and knelt down next to her. Anna immediately hid her face away under his arm, just as she had that time at the hunting-lodge. Sven understood that she had found herself a refuge and tempting her out would be no easier than it was with a wary forest animal. Anna's timidity was incomprehensible to him, but the more timid she became, the more coolly confident he felt himself. He cautiously embraced her, stroked her hair, shoulders and back; if she shuddered at his touch, he at once withdrew his hand and began all over again with a light caressing of her hair. So passed minute after minute, with them still kneeling on the floor in front of the open suitcase, Sven unable to see Anna's eyes or face. But he did not attempt to hurry her; there was no need for that.

Sven had had, in his thirty years, a fair amount of experience with women. There had been casual student liaisons as well as more serious attachments. He had even married, but it had not worked out and soon led to an amicable divorce. Sometimes he was at ease with women, sometimes the reverse. At times he had not been at his best at moments of initial intimacy. Up till now he had been afraid that such might be the case with him and Anna – she was so full of boldness and decision. But now as he held her body, trembling with, to him, unaccountable fear, and knowing that she sought defence against that fear not in her own strength of will but in him and only in him, he felt himself to be a man as never before.

If Anna had been able to reason she could still not have explained her sudden access of shyness. Expressed in it was the loneliness of these last years, when she had dinned into herself by force of will that no kind of love awaited her in the West. She had not had and did not want adventurous affairs and consequently tried to look on men only as friends or colleagues. She had, however, heard a good many conversations turning on the affairs and liaisons of others. Sometimes Russian men would

111

confess, in the course of frank conversation, that they had only experienced the sexual side of life to the full with Western women. But what it was that they experienced exactly remained a secret with seven locks and she had no urge to find out. While on the journey she had wondered, when it came to the crucial point with her and Sven, whether she would behave like a country bumpkin. She had dismissed the thought, somehow unaware that the time was inexorably drawing near and that they would be alone at length, and not in a car on the autobahn...

At least an hour passed. Anna realized that no assault was being contemplated, and relaxed. She would have liked to free herself from Sven's arms, but she thought of how very cold the room was and clung to him, her own arms tight around him. Sven positioned himself more comfortably on the floor and, seating Anna on his knees, began rocking gently. She relaxed totally and even began to drowse, tired out by her anxiety. Hearing her even breathing, Sven whispered:

'That's it. We're already going to sleep. But it won't do on the floor.'

He rose carefully with Anna in his arms and carried her to the bed. He wanted to leave her for a moment and get undressed, but Anna, still without opening her eyes, drew him to her:

'Don't go far, I'm cold without you.'

'I'm only taking my things off ...'

'I'll do that.'

She set about undoing the buttons on his shirt, at the same time seeking his lips with hers.

It was so wonderful together, better than it had ever been with anyone else. At least it seemed so to them. Afterwards Anna really did fall asleep, and Sven lay beside her, perfectly calm and happy, waiting for her to wake.

She woke up when it was already getting dark in the room.

'Sven, I feel awfully like ...'

'So do I!' he interrupted and pulled her to him.

And this time, he sensed ecstatically that Anna, all fear

totally put aside, gave herself fully into his power, responding with joy to his every movement, not attempting for an instant to impose anything of her own.

Later, lying a little way from him so as to cool down, Anna began to laugh:

'Actually I wasn't meaning to say that. I wanted to say I felt awfully like eating ...'

'Little greedy.'

'That's not true! I'm a big greedy. Could you go down and ask the landlady for some milk?'

'Of course. What a wonderful idea, Annie!'

Anna smiled at Sven's new name for her, Annie. Well, severe 'Anna' wan't a name that suited her now.

Sven got dressed and went below. He returned after about ten minutes, sat down on the bed and took Anna by the hand.

'We'll have to go back to the restaurant you know. The landlady told me they're not allowed to sell milk. The radiation got here too.'

The radiation situation on the western borders of the USSR is normal, radiation levels have remained steady in the Ukraine and White Russia.

Radio Mayak, 11 May 1986, 21–00

As is generally known, in the period between 1971 and 1984, there were 151 accidents at nuclear power-stations in fourteen countries, without any reaction from Washington of this sort.

Pravda, 4 May 1986

Nuclear energy cannot be halted. It will develop.

Pravda, 7 May 1986

We will not deny that among the letters received in this office, there are those which express a negative attitude to nuclear energy.

Pravda, 2 June 1986

CHAPTER 12

Anastasia visits a Kiev hospital and the Party Provincial Committee

They refused to talk to Anastasia in the Provincial Health Department and when Alexey managed to get in to see the Ukraine Minister of Health, a deputy recognized him and grinned:

'Now then, Comrade Petrenko, do you really think we'd forgotten all about your foreign connections? Of course you won't get any information about Chernobyl victims here! As for you, Comrade Lebedeva, you'd best go back to Leningrad and wait for your relatives to get in touch with you themselves. If all the relations of our patients come flooding in from all over the country for an interview, we're not going to have time to do our work. One must have patience and restraint.'

Anastasia was upset but the cool reception from the health officials in no way discouraged Alexey.

'I never expected anything else from them, now we'll try another way.'

He led Anastasia along the ministry corridors and into someone's waiting-room. There they were met by a middle-aged secretary.

'Alexey Ivanovich, I am pleased to see you. My boss isn't here, he's in the province.'

'Your boss couldn't help me anyway. It's you I want to see, Vera Petrovna. I'm in trouble and I need help.'

'Alexey Ivanovich, sweetheart, I'd do anything for you! Tell me then, what's up?'

Vera Petrovna noted all the details down on a piece of

paper as she listened. Then she looked pensively at Anastasia.

'I won't say this is going to be easy. Still, you know what I owe to you, Alexey Ivanovich. So sit yourself down in the corner there while I get glued to the phone. It's lucky my boss isn't here today.'

Anastasia and Alexey sat in the visitors' chairs as Vera Petrovna dialled the first number.

'City Hospital, Number One? Ministry of Health here, Comrade Alexandrov's secretary. Please could you let me know sharpish if you've got in your Chernobyl section a certain Alena Prikhotko ... from Pripyat. No? Thanks, bye-bye.'

She rang round all the hospitals in City and Province while Anastasia studied her face, trying to guess the answer before Vera Petrovna spoke it aloud. The secretary then rang the city of Gomel in the White Russian Republic.

'This is just in case, they've got their own patients from the White Russian area of the thirty-kilometre zone.'

As might have been expected, there were no casualties at all from Chernobyl and Pripyat in White Russia.

'So, what else have we got? Ah yes, the Children's Hospital. Hello, good morning, this is Alexandrov's office at the ministry. I need to find out as a matter of urgency whether you've got Anton and Alexey Prikhotko there, four years of age, twins from Pripyat. Could be, could be, and one of them ... Yes ... right ... yes, of course I realize. OK.'

Anastasia pricked up her ears and seized Alexey's hand in powerful excitement. He tapped it with his own to calm her and whispered: 'Easy now.'

'Yes ...' Vera Petrovna went on. 'Well now then, two comrades will be on their way to you just now: Doctor Petrenko and a relative who can identify the boy. Show them the patient. And thanks very much for the information. Bye-bye.'

'Well?'

'They've got a boy of four or five over there in deep shock. Nobody's enquired about him and he's said nothing

116

himself. You'll have to go over there. You'll be able to identify your nephew?'

'Well, of course. I saw them last year. They can't have changed that much.'

'Not in a year but in these days a lot of people have changed so much they hide them from their mothers ... I hope this doesn't turn out to be one of your nephews.'

'Who's that nice lady, Alyosha?' asked Anastasia when they were outside.

'She's the mother of a boy I operated on. It was a success, one of those I'm proud of to this day.'

Half an hour later Alexey and Anastasia were entering the Children's Hospital. The chief physician took them into the Chernobyl children's section. Anastasia had been in regional children's hospitals on occasion, visiting sick pupils. Any children's hospital is an oppressive experience for visitors, but the impressions are softened by the cheerful voices of children who are getting better.

Here there was total silence in the corridor and in the wards they passed.

They arrived in the intensive care ward. Children of various ages lay in the beds. Next to several were drip-feeds of blood and various solutions. A nurse sat knitting on a chair in the corner.

'And here's the boy I spoke about on the phone.'

In a cot by the window a boy was lying. Even in a child's bed he seemed too small for his four years. His little face was emaciated, his head shaven. His left hand was bandaged to a small stool placed nearby and the dropper needle was inserted in the vein. He was having a blood transfusion.

'Third transfusion but his own just won't rise,' whispered the doctor. 'Well, does he belong to you?'

Anastasia came nearer to the boy and called softly:

'Antosha! ... Alyosha!'

The boy evinced no reaction. His eyes were closed.

'Well?' asked the chief physician.

'He's in such a state it's hard to tell,' whispered Anastasia. 'The hair's so short, you can't tell the colour.'

'It hasn't been cut. It fell out.'

'If only he would open his eyes.'

The doctor stooped over the boy and tickled him under the chin with one finger. The dark-blue lids darted open for an instant to let Anastasia glimpse the cherry-stone eyes, dark as if they too were filmed over in dark blue.

With an anguished sigh, she shook her head.

'No, that's not our boy. Ours had bright-blue eyes – eye colour can't change can it?'

'No, not to that extent. Well then. I can be glad for you.'

They left the ward on tiptoe.

After lunch, which passed in an oppressive silence, Anastasia and Tatyana set off for the Provincial Committee.

To begin with, on learning that Anastasia was a headmistress from Leningrad Province they were made welcome and directed to one of the secretaries. He let them in out of turn, though there were a good dozen people in the waiting-room.

Slim, on the young side, the secretary was clearly one of the Gorbachev breed and began at once, business-like and practical:

'I'm told you're here about the Chernobyl accident. Fire away, I'll answer any questions you like. We have nothing to hide, we're ready to give full information. There's no shame in misfortune, it must be fought against. It should be said that on that front, if everything is not yet in order, at least there is total overall preparedness to achieve the elimination of all the effects of the accident and put things to rights inside the zone and the province as a whole. I'm sorry, you're here from which organization?'

'I'm here on my own account, no organization. But I've been in the party fifteen years. So if you like, I'm from the party organization. My question, though, is purely personal.'

'Right. Understood,' the secretary brought out, somewhat disappointed. 'Well now, a personal question is also a party question. You know the emphasis being placed on the human factor everywhere nowadays.'

'I am not a human factor. I'm just a person. My sister and her children have disappeared without trace. Can you help me to find them?'

'People disappeared without trace when there was a war

118

on. We've had an accident, so let's drop the hysterical expressions. Tell me who your sister is.'

Anastasia told him, adding her own itinerary of unsuccessful efforts.

After listening to her reasonably closely the secretary fell to thinking. He picked up a weighty folder from his desk and rocked it on his palms.

'You know what I have here?'

'Applications for lost relatives?'

'No. In this file are applications for party membership written by those who are now working to eliminate the effects of the accident. Among them are power-station workers and not all of them know where their wives and children are. But they're not writing about that, they urgently want membership of the Communist Party of the Soviet Union. Why do you think they feel that has greater priority?'

Anastasia shrugged.

'Well then, I'll tell you. Because they believe, you understand, they believe. They believe that the state and the party will not abandon their relatives in their misfortunes, wherever they are. And you, a party member for fifteen years, race about from Leningrad to Moscow and Kiev spreading panic along the way, distracting doctors, distracting party and state employees from working for the good of all the people who suffered in the accident! All of them! Your relatives included. That's all I have say. The rest you can read in the newspapers. You know we have a new policy, our press prints only what's true.'

'So what did your press print the last seventy years of Soviet power, a pack of lies?'

'Now don't go over the top. You shouldn't, you a party member for fifteen years.'

'Yes, fifteen years. And for all those years I believed the party. Now I don't believe a single word any more. Just because of your newspapers. You've lied your heads off over Chernobyl. You write one thing today and tomorrow it will be something else.'

'Do you realize what you're saying? For words like that...'

'What, I should be shot?'

'Expelled from the party, that's what. I shall inform Leningrad Province what you're up to here: spreading panic, slandering Soviet authority. You shouldn't be allowed within sight of a school. You have been entrusted with the education of the rising generation, but you...'

The secretary got up from his desk, like a purple colossus, eyes flashing lightning, the thunder of authority in his voice. Anastasia was not cowed. She took her party card from her handbag and walked directly up to the secretary. He stepped back and sat down in his chair again, as if propelled into its leathery depths by her look.

'You can denounce me to the Leningrad Province Party,' Anastasia pronounced quietly and clearly, 'and attach this to your report.'

She placed the card on the desk and left the office. In the waiting-room she saw an agitated Tatyana and a pale lady-secretary. Tatyana seized her under the arm and led her out into the corridor.

'What happened in there, Nastenka? We could hear you both shouting in the waiting-room.'

'Wait a moment, let me get my breath back ...' Anastasia was gasping, holding her hand to her heart.

'Are you all right? Let's have a sit-down in the cafe, it's on the first floor here.'

'No thanks, I've had enough of these top-brass corridors, offices, coffee and caviare. Let's go home.'

On the way, somewhat calmer, Anastasia went over everything which had occurred in the secretary's office, for the benefit of her friend. Then she asked, worried:

'You and Alexey won't get into trouble over me?'

'More trouble?' smiled Tatyana. 'Really we've got used to it. He's a doctor, I'm a teacher, we can find work somewhere else. We'll advertise. "Exchange, two-room flat in Kiev for one room any other city. Hiroshima and Nagasaki need not apply." Incidentally, Alexey returned his party card as well two years ago. He didn't talk to them about it though. He sent it through the post.'

That evening when Alexey returned from work all three discussed the events of the day over tea.

'You know, there's one thing I don't understand. What are they afraid of? In all this cover-up, newspaper lying, hysterics over Western opinion, the insolent way they talk to people, beneath all this aggression there's a sense of underlying fear. All over the place, here, Moscow, in the press ...' remarked Anastasia.

Alexey looked at her thoughtfully.

'What are they afraid of? Really they're not worried about panic, they're afraid of any kind of unexpected reaction. On the one hand each one is afraid of the rank above him. Don't think this accident won't claim victims among the top brass. They'll roll, they'll roll, those little party heads! It's just now at the start that it looks as if all necessary measures were taken at once, everyone stayed at their posts and led the rescue work like heroes. I don't think! There's some bosses haven't been found to this day. By the way, there were one or two doctors took off without saying goodbye. The ones who ran of course were those who knew best what sort of accident it was and what the real dangers were, to their own health I mean. Why on earth shouldn't they fear panic among ordinary folk if experts lost their heads? More than panic though, they were afraid of people's anger. Nobody knew how fathers would behave if they knew how a dose of radiation would affect their children in the future. So the powers that be have done everything to put a damper on it, first by total silence, then the sudden evacuation under the supervision of the police and now this torrent of reassuring news. You know the Kiev journalists' joke?'

'I know it,' smiled Tatyana. 'You tell Anastasia.'

'The journalists started this joke: "Reporting from Chernobyl. The radiation situation at the Chernobyl nuclear power-station is stabilizing, the radiation situation is stabilizing ... situation is stabilizing ... situation is stab- ... Doctor!" ... "Dear listeners, after a short break, another correspondent will continue our report. He will be telling you about how the situation at Chernobyl has already stabilized."'

'You mean people still have the courage to make jokes about such things?' Anastasia was astonished.

'Now Nastenka, you must surely remember that most Soviet jokes, if they're not about women, are always about serious matters or our own dear authorities. You remember the one about Brezhnev not only collecting foreign cars but jokes about himself as well – three camps full. Remember?'

'No, I don't. My sister Anna was the one for that sort of thing. Incidentally, my friends, now that we're in it up to the neck, may I book a call to Stockholm from here to talk to Anna? She might still be there and if she's gone back to Germany they'll give me her phone number.'

'Why ask? Give me the number, I'll book it,' said Tatyana.

While waiting for the call, everyone had more tea. To drive away gloomy thoughts, Anastasia asked:

'Now then, cheerful Kievans, what other jokes are going around about Chernobyl?'

'Well, they're all mostly professional. The weather forecasters, for example, say this: "We are broadcasting the weather forecast for April 26th. In Kiev a little low cloud, no rain, day temperature 24–26 degrees, night 16–18. Vinnitsa, clear, temperature 22–24 degrees. Chernobyl 2000 degrees, cloudy." Those people who've been inside the zone have brought two slogans back: "To the militaristic explosion in Nevada, we reply with a peaceful atomic explosion in Chernobyl!" and the other one: "Atoms for peace – in every home!"'

'And listen to this one from the kids where one of my friends works,' Tatyana broke in. 'It's a joke fairy-tale: "A cottage-loaf is rolling through the wood when a fox comes along. 'Cottage-loaf, cottage-loaf, I'm going to eat you up.' 'I wouldn't advise it, I'm not a cottage-loaf, I'm a hedgehog from Chernobyl.'" And the senior boys drew a new coat of arms for Kiev – a cockerel with two heads. Ukrainians are called cockerels to tease them, you know.'

They laughed grimly and then fell into a cheerless silence.

'Yes, stories like that,' Alexey went on pensively, 'are a sign of utter despair, the impossibility of fighting your own trouble with your own effort, just like the ancients at the mercy of fate, though the authorities play the role of fate here.'

'No, I don't agree.' Tatyana struck the arm of her chair with her fist. 'No! While people can laugh over the most awful troubles, it means they're still conscious of themselves. It's just been driven down into their subconscious and breaks out in the form of these jokes, folk songs and today's black humour.'

'The people's natural subconscious?' smiled Alexey, 'that's a new one.'

'Yes, yes and don't argue with me, you, you old pessimist!'

'A pessimist, little mother, is merely a well-informed optimist. Don't forget where I work these days.'

'Yes. Just your luck to transfer to an emergency post at the right time. What do you think about it, Nastenka? Does a folk subconscious exist? If a people are not just a collection of individuals, a sum of units, but a whole organism, how can it be simpler than an individual human organism? The mechanism of its life must be much more complicated than our leaders reckon.'

'Actually you're right. And if we conceive that people and authority are not one whole, that "people" and "party" are not "united" as the slogans bawl at every street corner, it follows that they are two different and antagonistic organisms. The subconscious terror of the authorities at any spontaneous, uncontrolled movement of the popular organism becomes easier to understand. Like now for instance.'

'Two different organisms, you say . . .' Alexey pondered. 'As a medical man, I can think of another comparison. Not two different organisms, just one sick organism – society, eaten up by uncontrolled cellular growth. Malignant tumour. And however much you rearrange or modify, a cancer remains a cancer.'

'How can you cure such a society, then? By operating?'

'Well, no, although I'm a cardiologist, not a cancer specialist, even I know that in this condition surgical intervention is contra-indicated. Metastases. There are two ways in this case. The first is careful, well-thought-out therapy.'

'The second?' asked Anastasia, now animated.

'The second – is a miracle.'

'A miracle!' Tatyana was amazed. 'Is that you talking, atheist?'

'I'm not an atheist, Tanechka. I don't deny there's a God at all. I simply don't know, but I fully admit the possibility that there is something, hidden from my perception and understanding. I admit in medicine as well there's a lot of things I don't know and can't understand, though I do know a thing or two in medicine. To deny God requires a conviction that He doesn't exist. I don't have any information on the non-existence of God. To believe blindly in His absence, well that would mean being a religious person, just inside-out. No, either give me clear proof, preferably strictly scientific, or I have to feel some sort of inner unproven conviction. Well, like I don't have to prove I love Tanechka or that she's the finest woman in the world. I wouldn't undertake to prove it but I believe all right – any monk or hermit would envy my belief in that!' Whereupon he kissed his wife quickly.

'Get away with you.' Tatyana brushed him away, flattered in spite of herself. 'You always turn any serious conversation into a joke.'

'Still, what is the second way to cure it, the miracle?' asked Anastasia, looking at them and smiling.

'Miracle? Well it actually happened with a famous cancer specialist. Actually there had been a number of such cases in his experience, but I know of one. They brought an old woman to his clinic suffering from cancer of the stomach and intestine. He started to reassure her before they irradiated her, but the old woman says to him: "Don't bother reassuring me, dear, I know I've got cancer and it's incurable." The professor didn't lose his head, just examined her and said: "Well, mother, I was going to write cancer in your records. Why are you trying to pull my leg? Just tell me, have you eaten a lot of sauerkraut?" "Well, what a question, what else do you eat in the country during the winter except potatoes and sauerkraut?" the old wife answered. "Course I have, deary, a lot of cabbage in my life." So he washes his hands and says sternly: "Your

124

cabbage is what's poisoning you. I'll have to give you some treatment but I wouldn't have had to if it wasn't for your own foolishness. But only if once I've cured you, you don't eat a mouthful of that cabbage any more! Otherwise, no treatment!" He talked about that cabbage so much, the old wife believed him and because of her faith, she upped and recovered. Most people know miracles like that in the history of medicine. And what about you, language and literature specialist,' he glanced quizzically at Anastasia, 'do you believe in miracles?'

'I believe in the power of the human spirit. Spirit, not factor.'

'Brrr... What a word to think up, "the human factor". I can imagine a weird sort of fairy-story: "Out of the cave came a Human Factor with six legs and twelve tongues and it spoke with a human voice."'

All three laughed and at that moment the telephone rang.

'Did you book Stockholm? Subscriber on the line,' sounded the insolent voice of the operator.

'Hello ... Annushka,' said Anastasia, pressing the receiver to her ear – the line was terrible – crackling and distant voices weaving in and out. A lady answered, the one who had come to the phone last time. She was the first to speak.

'Hello! Why haven't you phoned? Annushka's already gone back to Germany.'

'I see ... How can I get in touch with her then?'

'Very simple. Write down her telephone number.' She dictated it.

'It's a little town somewhere in the Alps. Annushka's there with Sven having a holiday after her trip here!'

'Sven? Who is he, may I know?'

'He's Annushka's' – a pause – 'fiancé.'

'Really? I didn't know she had a fiancé. Well, all right, thank you.'

'Wait a minute, don't hang up. Tell me about Alenushka, have you found her yet? We're all terribly worried about her.'

'No, I've found nobody so far. Thank you for the number ... and the news.'

125

'Not at all, not at all! If you need me, please don't hesitate to ring, I can pass everything on to Anna. I'll ring her straight away and tell her you called.'

'Then you know what we could do? If it's no trouble, give her my number in Kiev. I won't try to contact her from here then, it's pretty complicated. By the way, what is your name?'

'Faina Borisovna Carlsson. Right, give me the number, otherwise the units will be mounting up, I know only too well.'

Anastasia dictated the Kiev number and after saying goodbye and thanking her breezy partner, hung up, shaking her head and shrugging.

'Well, Anna! You know what she's up to while I'm looking for her sister here? Getting married! She's got a fiancé there, Sven they call him.'

Tatyana smiled and stroked Anastasia's arm.

'Nastenka, you're our proper and severe person again. You mustn't be! They didn't tell you about the wedding, did they, they just said she had a fiancé.'

'Even if there was a wedding,' Alexey added, 'would that be the end of the world? I'm invited to a wedding in a village where they took the evacuees from Chernobyl and Pripyat. You remember Tanechka, Sergei Kuzmich, our old radiologist? When he retired, he went to his daughter in Chernobyl. They bought a house with a nice garden; Kuzmich got hold of a little boat and thought he'd end his days fishing and cultivating strawberries. And now this ... And today he suddenly rings me up from Ivankov and invites me to a wedding at the house he's at, some people called Yevdokimov own it. You could tell by his voice the wedding's not going to be a jolly affair. Still...'

'Are you going?' asked Tatyana.

'Certainly. He was keen for me to go, and anyway I've got some tests to do not far from there, just off my way really.'

'Alexey!' Anastasia roused herself, 'take me with you. What if Alenka's with them?'

'Well there's not much chance of that, there's tens of

thousands of them round Ivankov. I could make enquiries on my own, if it comes to that.'

But Anastasia, hands clenched, was looking at him with such imploring eyes, that he relented.

'OK, Nastenka. We'll go together. You can be my lab technician and help me do the tests. We'll imagine you've decided to change your profession, like me.'

'Well, if it helps me to get near to Alenka I'll come and be your lab technician or charwoman or whatever. If I could only get into the zone to find some trace of her!'

'Don't talk nonsense. Nobody's going to let you into the zone and there're no traces there anyway, they took them all away. There's no point in going. The charwomen there are soldiers and robot-bulldozers. Well, if you really want to come with me tomorrow, go and have a proper shower and have an early night.'

'Thanks ever so much. I have a feeling that tomorrow I'll find out something about Alenka. And thanks to you, Tanechka.'

She went off meekly to the shower, obediently washed her hair and then lay down in the bed Tatyana had made. She went to sleep at once.

There has never been a power-station like it in our area. Quite a number of technical methods will be employed here for the first time, that's why we are experimenters. The construction rate is unusual, judge for yourselves, as early as the end of the five-year plan the first turbines will be installed. The industrial atom of Poles'ye will breathe new strength into the life of our green land!

Journal Navka i suspilstvo No.11 1971

During the first tense and anxious days I was working at Poles'ye. Here at the main Regional Hospital, a centre for special assistance was organized. Patients being treated there displayed an astonishing understanding of the situation, a high level of tact, even nobility. Those whose illnesses were not too serious asked to be released from the hospital. They gave up their beds to those most seriously affected by the accident at the power-station.

V. Kozlyuk,
employee Ukraine Ministry of Health
Izvestiya, 7 May 1986

Those present at the meeting between diplomatic representatives and the chairman of the Ukraine Council of Ministers A. Lyashko displayed interest in the discrepancy in figures – 92,000 evacuated and more than 220,000 people undergoing special medical investigation. This is explained by the fact that now special attention is being given to any person who goes to his doctor complaining of feeling unwell.

Izvestiya, 23 May 1986

In all 135,000 people have been evacuated from the Chernobyl region.

Moscow Radio on the press conference at
the USSR Ministry of Internal Affairs
21 August 1986, 19–00

Here cowards were sharply shown up and new heroes born. The power-station accident will not only be a cruel technical lesson for us but also a moral lesson.

Pravda Ukraine, 8 May 1986

Up till now certain Komsomols from the 'Jupiter' factory in Pripyat have not advised their whereabouts. They're obviously sitting it out somewhere like mice, waiting for things to quieten down here.

Pravda, 23 May 1986

In all the Pripyat Party organization has on record 2,611 communists. Up till now the whereabouts of 2,434 have been established.

Pravda, 3 July 1986

The former management of the station have been relieved of their responsibilities. The former director of the station V. Bryukhanov and the chief engineer N. Fomin in the complex accident situation were unable to furnish proper firm leadership and essential discipline. They displayed irresponsibility and mismanagement. At the most critical moment the deputy director R. Solovyov abandoned his post. Deputy directors I. Tsarenko and V. Gundar failed to display the necessary responsibility to their duties. A section of the power-station employees are still 'on the run'.

Pravda, 15 June 1986

Kiev and the Ukraine have responded to the events at Chernobyl with a powerful wave of humour. Witty, salty remarks are especially appreciated by people who have to work in the danger zone.

Literary Gazette, 4 June 1986

CHAPTER 13

Anastasia talks to driver Kolya about the evacuation and about life in general

Anastasia woke well before dawn. As soon as it began to grow light in the room, she got up from her folding bed and went barefoot into the kitchen. She took out a bottle of mineral water from the fridge to make the coffee, some eggs, and began to prepare breakfast, keeping an impatient ear open for the alarm-clock in her hosts' room.

At half past six, she and Alexey at last left the house.

'We'll get to the emergency station early while there are none of my colleagues about,' Alexey had told her over breakfast. 'I don't want any unnecessary questions. I'll leave a note for the management that I'm out doing tests in the rural areas and that'll be that. Main thing is to get a document written out for you. Yes, and we mustn't forget a gown for you – make it more convincing. There's strict control everywhere, check-points all over the place. Well, it's all right, we'll make it OK.'

'If we get the chance can we go to Chernobyl?'

'Well no, you can only go there, or into the zone at all, with a special pass. Even the Moscow film boys haven't been allowed in yet. They wanted to do a newsreel but the bosses here wouldn't have it – not surprisingly. Anyway we don't need to go into the zone, there's nobody there except people sorting out the accident. You have to look for Alenka in the places they took the evacuees. And that's where we're going.'

At the emergency station they spent nearly an hour. Alexey wrote out travel passes for Anastasia and himself and wangled a car and driver. The necessary maps were found.

'Our driver's a reliable man and knows the score,' whispered Alexey as they made their way towards a 'Uazik'. 'He took part in the evacuation himself, ferrying people. He's got a sceptical attitude towards the powers that be and knows how to keep his mouth shut. He's called Kolya.'

Kolya turned out to be a husky man in his forties with the look of a benevolent drunk.

'Which way, chief? The sea?'

'That's it, Kolya. We'll do some tests, then on to the areas.'

'The sea' was Kievans' name for their reservoir, Anastasia guessed. They got there quite quickly. Alexey took the sample bottles and went down to the green evil-smelling water while Kolya and Anastasia settled down to wait for him on the shore road.

'Alyosha was saying that you helped in the evacuation of the accident area?' asked Anastasia, who was dying to know how it had all gone.

'Yes. I carried folk out. There weren't enough bus-drivers at the depot, so they called us up.'

'Is it true what they say in the papers, that the evacuation started two hours after the accident?'

'Tripe,' responded Kolya coolly and lit up a papirosa. 'What's your interest, or are you just curious? To be honest I'm not fond of people who are just curious.'

'I've got a reason, Kolya. Ever since the first days of the accident I've been looking for my sister. Her husband worked at the station. She's got two boys and she's expecting another child. Her husband's dead, he died of radiation in Moscow.'

'A bad do. It was such a mess all round, plenty of people got split up. Plenty haven't found each other yet. Still, what do you expect when you know what a rush-job they did?'

'Could we sit down, Kolya, and you can tell me how it went?'

Kolya smiled indulgently.

'And just where were you thinking of sitting? The grass was it? So first we've got to call Alexey Ivanovich with the dosimeter, so he can test the grass, otherwise your backside would get singed before long, not to mention more important things. Away into the car.'

They got in and Kolya placed both arms on the wheel to rest his head on.

'You're asking about the evacuation ... Well, I can tell you what I saw myself, where I was myself. They called me on the morning of April the 27th and said: "You're going to Pripyat with a convoy. Get ready." We left in the morning, stretched out over several kilometres. As we go, we see check-points all round but we get through without a murmur. We got to Pripyat but not right into the place. They dispersed us so we wouldn't seem too obvious from the settlement. We were told to wait till the people were got ready to evacuate. So we got out to stretch our legs a bit and we were amazed: seemed like the people knew nothing about any evacuation! The boys were hard at it playing football, wives hanging the washing out to dry, a fisherman on his way back from the river with a bucket. He'd caught some radioactive fish and was pleased about it, but had nobody to tell...'

'What was the matter? Didn't anybody hear the explosion? They weren't all deaf, were they?'

'But the explosion was in the block itself you see. It could be heard, but only just. The only people who knew about it were the ones in the station. Well, after that, they spread us round the town in front of the houses, by the entrance. Police were brought in to make a cordon round all the houses at once. Just like paratroopers taking a town. People were running to their houses but the cops grabbed them and forced them into the buses in what they had on. Then they started bringing the people out of the houses. Some came by themselves, some leaning on each other. The wives set up a howl: "I'm not going without my husband", another one crying, her children were out playing, where were they taking her without her children? Didn't matter, everybody bunged into the buses without explanation. Some smart mams dressed the children for travelling, others brought them out in short trousers, it being a hot day, you see. Some of them wanted to take stuff with them

133

and came out with bags and cases, the most efficient people. Well, they told them to drop them, take nothing with them: "Evacuation's only for a day or two. Everything will be ready for you when we get there." I was already trying not to look, my hands were shaking enough already: well it was as if they were dealing with dumb cattle. They were all scared of a panic so they tried to grab people any old how, so nobody had time to think or ask questions.

'Yes ... well we drove them off where we were told. The convoy crawls slowly along; behind, kids are howling, wives weeping, menfolk swearing. I've driven plenty in my time, I've sat behind a wheel in the north, in the camps, I've been in accidents but I've never had a trip like that one. Well, we dropped them off at different places...'

'Which places exactly?'

'Some here, some there. Roughly speaking the first trip was to the Poles'ye and Ivankov areas. But they were split up again after that: one bus here, one bus there. And straight away the mix-up started. The first ones to be dropped were mothers with children and those toddlers who'd been brought along without any parents, from kindergartens and creches. No sooner had we set people down when the cry goes up straight away: "Where are my children? Where've they taken my wife?" At the various places the police and local authorities met them and whisked them off to the houses of the locals. The orders to them were: "Like it or not you've got to take in one evacuated family and get them settled." Well, you have to say, our wives are tender-hearted, they were really loving towards the evacuees and took them round their huts. Not all of course, there were plenty who threatened to complain, wouldn't let people in their houses: "They've got the plague on them, radiation! They'll give it to my kids. They can't come in and that's final." Well those were shut up pretty quickly. All of them got sorted out either by the police or the local authorities. I was standing there when the chairman in one village threatened to take one man's house away if he didn't take a family in. I don't know how the evacuees are going to get on with them. Still you can understand people: it's not wartime after all, not so easy to let some strange mob into your house, with kids to feed and settle in. That's the way our authorities thought – shove all the work on somebody else to start with, sort it out later.'

'I don't quite follow you, Kolya. If they took out so many people at once, however many thousands, where could they put them all? Obviously there was no other way of doing it.'

Kolya raised his head and turned abruptly towards her.

'No other way? Well, us drivers got together over a glass, talking about if there was another way that would be easier on folk.'

'And did you find one?'

'Course we did. Straight away. Just listen. To begin with, on the first day they didn't evacuate the whole ninety thousand, just the people from Pripyat, the energy settlement and a few from Chernobyl. We took people out at night after that, from there. I'm not talking about the other places; out of the fifteen-kilometre zone – the thirty zone came later, we were making trips for nine days, the drivers told me, and a policeman I know. They were in no hurry at all about the thirty-kilometre zone, so they would hardly take them, not all at once. So. Round the province there's no fewer than 1,001 pioneer camps, empty just now – the holidays haven't started yet, d'you see. So they could have distributed people round these empty camps, and housed them where all the worry wouldn't have been pushed on to the locals. Did the lads get it right, then?'

'Actually, yes. But why didn't the authorities think of that?'

'Maybe they did think of it, but it didn't suit their book. It's obvious why it didn't as well.'

'Why was that then?'

'Well the people had to be fed, didn't they – one. Then on the second or third day they could be put to work in the villages, go out to the collective farms – that's two. That's calculation for you. Does anyone care if it's less bother for folks some other way? No. But, mark my words, the evacuees won't all go back from the camps – I don't mean the pioneer camps either, I've heard tell they're already building camps for them next to small villages.'

'Why should they do that now? The papers say people will be back in their homes very soon.'

'To my way of thinking they won't be back all that soon. It'd be strange if this story was over soon; looks to me as if it's just starting. The authorities need to allocate people to permanent sites by winter, all in good time they'll build special settlements. D'you read the papers or listen to the radio?'

'Now and again. But I'm on the road most of the time. Anyway they write one thing one day and something else the next.'

'Well I see you don't know how to read the papers properly. Now if you read the papers properly every day and listened to the radio every day, you'd learn to read and hear more than they give you.'

'How do you mean exactly? Foreign radio, you mean?'

'Why foreign? Of course it does no harm to listen to hostile voices for the sake of comparison. Only a smart bloke can find out what he wants without any voices, when the radio and papers lie all the time.'

'Well – and how does he do it if they all lie?'

'You've got to learn to read between the lines and hear between the words. Now say I hear for example that some bunch of shock-workers in Petrozavodsk are working on an urgent contract for wooden prefabs for the evacuees, and later the newsreader joyfully announces that in a couple of months the people are going back to Chernobyl and Pripyat. Well I think to myself, they're not going back anywhere, they're going to be put somewhere out of the way in those little wooden houses. And if they've gone and ordered them in Petrozavodsk when there's a similar plant in the Carpathians nearer to us, it stands to reason that the Carpathian work-people couldn't cope, because they just need thousands and thousands of houses. Then they lie to me that none of the inhabitants got a dose of radiation. Let's say I know about this because I've ferried them round the hospitals plenty of times, these casualties, but say I believe them. Then I hear that eleven hundred medics are working with the evacuees, that's three hundred teams. And then I remember that with normal healthy people,

136

checking them once or twice, that would be no more than two days' work. So I draw my own conclusion: never mind how much you reassure the public, you've got enough radiation cases to keep you going. And I conclude: these wooden houses, and doctors from all corners of the Ukraine are needed because you want to keep these sick people isolated – one. You're settling people in the new areas for good – two. And you have to lie because things are really serious – three. So that's it, they lie and a smart bloke gets the truth out of them. See?'

'I suppose so. It's rather complicated for me though, I must confess, this way of gathering news.'

'Well naturally, what d'you expect from a woman? No don't get upset, I'm telling the truth, I can see you've had an education. Still, even if a woman gets to be a professor, she's still a woman and if she understands anything in this life, it's with her belly, not her head. Take politics, just tell me for instance, did you respect the authorities before Chernobyl?'

'Yes I did, Kolya. I'm a party member myself. Was,' added Anastasia quietly, almost to herself.

'Right. And now they've stuck a roasted cockerel up your arse, what's your opinion now? You realize the amount of bad things done and rubbish talked around this accident? And no imperialist sharks either – they swim in their own seas, our own sharks I mean. Has it sunk in yet that they don't give a toss about you and your sister and her kids, they've got their own worries – how can they get out of this business with clean hands and keep people's ears and mouths shut?'

'It's sunk in, Kolya.'

'Right. Just remember you didn't get to it with your mind though, it was your woman's insides did it. If you were a man, you'd need more brains than the rest to work it out. A man's got to sort out everything with his brain, so he gradually, little by little, starts to think and he might get as far as the truth. A woman now – she gets to know in a totally different way. To look at her she's a complete fool, understands nothing. Touch her heart though and she'll come out with things a professor couldn't manage. You did

137

right to look for your sister yourself. That's another example of our authorities' policy. When we get to Ivankov you'll see notes pinned up on the fences – people looking for relatives or children. On the radio meanwhile there's hours of chat about heroic firemen at the power-station and how everybody there's a hero. But no thought to give an hour's air-time for something useful: reading out those notes: "Seeking boy Yurochka, three years, fair hair, dressed in blue shirt and short red pants. Knows his own name."'

Kolya thumped his fist against the wheel and uttered an obscenity.

'Excuse the bad language, mother, but when I remember those notes ... and every week on the radio there's a programme where people are searching out relations lost sight of during the war. They're not scared of that today, that's past and gone. And what happened after the war? I was in a children's home myself, a military one. And I remembered my own name, I could talk and I even knew the address in Leningrad where we lived: Sennaya Square, number thirteen, flat sixty-one. When I grew up I went. No relatives there, some other people living there. The trouble was I couldn't remember my surname. Obviously my parents made me learn the address so I wouldn't get lost, but they didn't think about the surname. If they had broadcast even an hour-a-day search programme back then, I wouldn't have known my happy childhood at state expense, that I don't wish to remember. Well, never mind that ... Good for you, though, that you've found Alexey Ivanovich for the job. He's a clever bloke and he's got a heart. I'll put my oar in as well if I think of anything while I'm going around. As I understand it, we're off to Ivankov. Don't cry, little froggy, we shan't drown!'

Kolya clapped Anastasia on the shoulder after his own fashion and the friendly gesture put fresh heart into her. Her confidence had increased the nearer she got to finding the first traces of Alenushka.

Alexey came back with his water samples, got into the car and they set off along an empty beach drenched in sunshine. The water was deserted too; just in one corner of

138

the green expanse a motionless motor-ship gleamed white.

'*Academician Marzeyev*,' said Alexey, nodding in its direction. 'Floating laboratory. Keeping watch on the sluice-gates.'

'Why is it doing that?' asked Anastasia.

'If there's a sudden rise in radioactivity, the dam can be closed.'

'So there is a danger that the radiation could rise at any moment?'

'Of course there is, anything's possible ... in which case the water situation really is bad. We're on starvation water rations as it is.'

'Really? The water situation can't be as bad as that in the Ukraine, can it?'

'It certainly is, Nastenka. Even before Chernobyl our water was nineteen times less than the national average.'

'What, including the Central Asian Republics with deserts?'

'Yes, just imagine. That's the way we run things, dear. Nature doesn't like us. You've heard the motto of our meliorists? "Let us turn every swamp into a desert!" So there you are.'

'Where are we going?' enquired Kolya.

'Ivankov,' responded Alexey.

One can live within the thirty-kilometre zone even now. The evacuation was carried out there only because people should not be exposed to risk.

Pravda Ukraine, 8 May 1986

The inhabitants of the station settlement were evacuated in a matter of hours.

M. Gorbachev, speech on Central TV
14 May 1986, 21–00

The evacuation of the population commenced on April the 27th. Women and children were sent off first. Around 48,000 persons were evacuated from Chernobyl and adjacent areas within a radius of thirty kilometres. As a prophylactic measure, potassium iodide tablets were distributed to the population both within the thirty-kilometre zone and beyond it.

Survey of MAGATE representatives
APN, 12 May 1986

The fire is extinguished. But ahead lies a no less complex and important matter, requiring on the one hand tact and understanding, and on the other speed of completion. The matter concerns the evacuation. The police carried out their part well. The whole town of Pripyat was divided into five sectors, and five corresponding evacuation groups were set up. These were headed by the responsible officials of the town force of the Ukraine MVD. The Deputy Minister of Internal Affairs of the Ukraine, General G. Berdov, arrived in Pripyat on April the 26th and Major-General A. Borovik, head of the political section, on the 27th. They returned to Kiev only on May the 4th when the more complex operations had at length been carried out.

Izvestiya, 7 May 1986

On his arrival at dawn on April the 26th, General Berdov could not believe his eyes. On the left, a fiery glow over the industrial compound, while here with Saturday idleness the town was unhurriedly waking up. Shops were opening, the streets were filling up with

people. Dressed for summer, they were hurrying to get away into the countryside with their children ...
Thousands of carefree families in holiday mood, unaware of danger.

Socialist Industry, 16 May 1986

Police have blocked all roads to the nuclear power-station and the settlement. The immediate environs of the station are of course very picturesque and people used to enjoy relaxing here on their days off. And this day was in fact a Saturday. But these places of relaxation have become a danger zone, and police detachments, naturally, have closed off access to them.

Pravda Ukraine, 8 May 1986

A thousand buses were already assembled below the atom town. The convoy moved in at 1400 hours precisely. A vehicle stopped outside every communal entrance. Many people, simply not thinking the radiation could last long, came out lightly dressed.

Pravda Ukraine, 8 May 1986

The announcement of imminent evacuation of course alarmed people. A whole delegation appeared at the executive committee. General Berdov was detailed to meet the people and allay their fears. Gennadi Vasilievich came out in his General's uniform. Tall, grey-haired, calm, he was able to find the most appropriate words on the impending evacuation.

'Somebody tried to raise objections, but he was hushed up,' relates the General. 'People, albeit with difficulty, recognized the reality of the danger.'

Soviet Russia, 8 May 1986

Collection points were not organized, so as to avoid commotion and panic. And the desired effect was achieved.

Major General A. Borovik,
chief of political section MVD Ukraine
Izvestiya, 7 May 1986

Well, we got the alarm call. We formed up into a convoy and set off for the town of Pripyat. There were a great lot of vehicles, I don't know the exact figures. But there were more than a thousand cars and buses. I'm not including lorries and so on. There was no panic at all. Workers were on duty round the clock. Well I was out there twice. The first time then the second time. At night. We had to go at night mainly. But everywhere on the roads there was order, and discipline, everywhere ...

> Interview with driver Alexander Milevski
> *Radio Mayak*, 17 May 1986

Some parents brought out their kids in little short pants and lightweight shirts and even let them out of the entrance halls to play in the street. It was exasperating: has stupidity any limit?

> *Komsomolskaya Pravda*, 11 May 1986

The evacuation poured out thousands of vehicles on to the roads ... Those nine days spent in the Chernobyl power-station area became the toughest days in the lives of General Berdov and his colleagues.

> *Pravda Ukraine*, 8 May 1986

Fine. We don't feel anything. Everything's all right. (Evacuees in Obukhovichi village in answer to a correspondent's question on how they felt.)

> *Radio Kiev*, 8 May 1986, 00–00

There have been fish caught in the upper reaches of the Dnepr, Sozha and Pripyat which have actually been found to contain a certain quantity of radioactive substances.

> *Soviet White Russia*, 8 June 1986

In thirty-six hours the population of many villages has doubled. In houses supper has been laid for families increased to ten–twelve persons.

> *Soviet White Russia*, 8 May 1986

And there is Petro Artemenko in Blidcha village. Big house, own car, lives with an insolent swagger. He point-blank refused to accept any evacuees: he'd just painted the floors in his new house, they'd be spoiled, they'd bring dirt in, they might steal something in the flat ...

Pravda, 23 May 1986

In the first days of the evacuation she looked for her children. Thirteen toddlers had got lost. They had travelled separately from their parents who had been put into the nearest villages, not the towns. Lists were made out and pinned up, wherever possible telephone numbers were given. They rang round the village councils themselves.

Komsomolskaya Pravda, 11 May 1986

At present in fifty-two villages in ten areas of Kiev Province, living quarters for the population evacuated from Chernobyl are going up at full speed. Forty thousand workers sent from all corners of the republic are toiling literally round the clock. Building works are being deployed mainly near small and distant villages.

Silski Visti, 13 July 1986

By autumn in the dispersal areas in White Russia we will have built forty new settlements.

A. Grakhovski, Chairman,
Gomel Provincial Executive Committee
Pravda, 23 July 1986

You saw the situation in 'Fairytale' camp? Notes on the doors and fences. They're looking for relatives, wives and children. People did not know where their loved ones were but went on duty nevertheless.

Pravda, 2 June 1986

CHAPTER 14

Anastasia and Alexey attend a wedding

In Ivankov, the regional centre, Alexey ordered Kolya to drive straight to the Regional Committee of the Party. He knew that announcements concerning the search for relatives were pinned up on the available spaces in front of the office there. And true enough, white notices concerning missing wives and husbands, parents and children covered the committee doors, the adjoining fence and the trees in front of the building. Examining and reading each in turn, Anastasia caught sight of a sheet torn from a school exercise-book with slanting squares. In crooked childish handwriting was written: 'I'm looking for my Mam and Dad. Katya Samoilenko.'

There was nothing about any Alenka. Alexey gave Anastasia a page from his notebook. She requested a second one and wrote on one concerning her search for Alenka; the second referred to the request of the Chernobyl victim in the Moscow clinic for information on the whereabouts of his family.

After this they proceeded to the Regional Police Department. All the fences and trees around it were hung about with similar advertisements. Kolya turned out to have a pal in this department, an ordinary station policeman. He promised to look at the lists of evacuees in Ivankov Region and also ring Poles'ye where they'd taken people from Chernobyl and Pripyat as well. Afterwards he would come to the Yevdokimovs' house and report results. Anastasia left her advertisements outside the police building too.

Business over, they went on to the Yevdokimovs'.

Laden tables stood in the garden close to a wooden house with a mezzanine; the wedding was in full swing.

Alexey frowned:

'They shouldn't have arranged it out in the open ... still there's a different mood here from Kiev. People are tired of taking precautions. Life will out. Well, you'll see for yourself.'

Spotting Alexey, a thin old man with an elaborate white hair-style rose from the table.

'Ivanovich! So you did get away, well I really wasn't expecting you, you know!'

They embraced.

'Let me introduce my wife's friend from Leningrad. And this is Kolya, my driver.'

Anastasia was seated next to Kolya while her other neighbour turned out to be a rather bouncy dark-eyed lady of about her own age.

'What can I get you to eat? Some goose? Mutton? We've got plenty of meat now, they say it's dangerous, but we're killing them off like we did at home. There's no feed for them anyway ... aubergine? Why aren't you drinking to the bride and groom? Come on, drink up! Everybody's got to drink spirits now, it protects you against radiation, they all say ...'

Anastasia raised the tiny glass to her lips. It was home-made vodka and made her choke.

'You just have a sip of this stewed fruit! All the wives here used to be teetotallers, now they all drink moonshine and stewed fruit for protection. We can't get vodka here, there's a crusade against it. So we do what we can – toast the bride and groom, like we always used to.'

She tossed off her glass feverishly and bit into a fresh cucumber. Then she leaned over against Anastasia and began whispering:

'Oh my, the things people do, they're crazy – getting married all over. Like breaking a chain – they're off. In these parts, weddings are always in autumn, but this is the fourth since they were dumped on us from Chernobyl. What sort of children are going to come out, eh, you tell

146

me! Are they going to have square heads or what?'

Anastasia listened tolerantly to her neighbour, agreeing absently. She was going to help herself to lettuce from the vast bowl, but Alexey made a negative signal with his eyes, so she had a slice of pie which turned out to be delicious.

'Here come the Vareniki, dear guests, Varenichki!'

Some women emerged from the house bearing an enormous pot of curds filling the garden with its mouthwatering smell. 'Who wants cottage cheese with theirs? Who potato?'

Anastasia glanced questioningly at Alexey. He understood her and said loudly:

'Dear hostesses, who'll give me some potato with mine?'

Then Anastasia did the same, though it looked unfamiliar. But she enjoyed it. The potato was mixed with fried onion and fat.

Toasts were proposed to the young people and their parents. New guests arrived, so everybody drank to them as well. Then two young lads appeared with accordions and everyone joined in singing Russian and Ukrainian songs, followed by dancing. The host had specially watered his front lawn for that. Her neighbour whispered to Anastasia:

'We've got instructions to water wherever there's dust.'

Old and young leapt about. It was amusing to see boys in jeans wildly dancing the gopak along with the older guests. Then the chastushki began. As the guests got drunker, the verses got more risqué until they reached the very limit of decency.

A young man in sports trousers and faded blue vest jumped into the crowd of dancers.

'That's Shlik! Now he'll come out with something ...' giggled Anastasia's neighbour.

The boy raced wildly round the circle until, halting near the accordionists, he gave out in a despairing voice:

What a sorry tale I tell,
The girls all run from me like hell.
Here I sit still cursing at 'em –
I blame it on the 'peaceful atom'!

147

Laughter drowned out the words. Shlik went on, this time imitating a girl's voice:

> Pripyat is where my love was bred
> And things get tough when we're in bed;
> If his prick won't take the strain –
> MAGATE's where I complain!

The guests again laughed, glancing at the bride and groom. The latter paled and stood up.

'Now then, stop the music, the moonshine's getting cold.'

The accordionists broke off the chastushka accompaniment and moved over to the table with the dancers. The bride was furtively wiping away her tears. Shlik had disappeared somewhere.

'Why on earth did he have to sing that about the bride and groom?' Anastasia asked her companion.

'He doesn't give a damn, he's a desperado that one,' she replied and, eyes rounded, added in a loud whisper, 'He goes into the zone.'

'The zone? Why?'

'What d'you mean, why? There's houses and flats abandoned, just standing there. Well he goes in there with his mates and picks up what's lying about. He's picked up enough of them X-rays now, they checked him not long ago, he asked them to. He doesn't care how he lives or what he sings, hasn't done for ages.'

Anastasia began to do some hard thinking. Then she extricated herself from behind the table and went into the garden in search of Shlik.

She found him under the flowering cherries. He was surrounded by his own companions: the boys and girls sat in a circle and were singing softly to a guitar. Anastasia knew the tune; the boys at her school used to sing something similar. The words, however, were not the same. The guitarist sang:

> Dust is spreading over Europe,
> Mushroom cloud, not low and not so high...

148

then everyone joined in:

> Tablecloth, tablecloth,
> Strontium settling,
> Creeping under your gas-mask
> And everyone, everyone,
> Hopes for the best –
> That death will pass him by this once.

When the young people had finished, Anastasia approached them and touched Shlik on the shoulder.

'Young man, may I have a word with you?'

He glanced round and stared at her:

'You one of the new teachers? I don't remember seeing you before.'

'Nor could you. I'm from Leningrad and I'd like to talk to you on a most serious matter. Let's talk over here.'

Shlik, intrigued, led her away to another corner of the garden. There they sat down on a small bench near the barrel of water used for watering. From behind it neither the guests nor Shlik's friends were visible. The first thing Anastasia did was to get all the money she had with her out of her bag, she took off her watch and her earrings.

'That's all 1 have at the moment but I can send you more from Leningrad later. And I've got a sister in West Germany, so parcels from there are guaranteed. And now listen to what I want you to do...'

They talked for at least half an hour, then parted. Anastasia at once went to speak to Alexey.

'Where did you get to? Our friend from the police is here. I'm afraid he's got no news at all for you, though. You can assume that Poles'ye and Ivankov regions have been checked: your people aren't there.'

'I knew how it would be, Alyosha. And now I have a great favour to ask you. Don't ask me any questions, just leave me here for a couple of days. It's business. It looks as if there's one more possibility and I'm going to make use of it.'

'You can't tell me about it?'

'No, I can't. A certain person has promised to help me to find out something about Alenka. As to how – that's his secret and not mine.'

Alexey thought deeply. Then he took Anastasia by the hand.

'Nastenka, I didn't want to worry you but I don't like the state you're in. For that reason I don't want to leave you on your own, who knows what ... But promise me at least that when you come back to Kiev, you'll agree to an electro-cardiogram.'

'I promise, Alyosha. But don't you worry: my heart will hold out as long as it needs to. I know myself.'

'Well, be careful. And look after yourself. When shall I come for you?'

'Tomorrow evening, can you?'

'What d'you mean? I'll be here.'

'Well we can go back to the table now. Although this wedding reminds me more of a wake...'

But the wedding continued.

Agricultural workers near the Chernobyl power-station are working more effectively than ever.

Pravda Ukraine, 8 May 1986

Thirty kilometres from the power-station, life proceeds as normal. Everything goes on as usual. Even weddings.

Soviet Russia, 18 May 1986

'We took in 2,100 persons from Chernobyl, here in Rozvazhnoye village. And very very pleased to do so.'

'I wonder about the young people.'

'All right. There's weddings here, people getting married.'

'When was this?'

'May the 9th, Victory Day.'

'They chose a very good day.'

'The people round here are tough, they don't panic, they're not scared, they're survivors.'

'They're panicking in New York, though.'

'Let them, sods. Here it's entirely the opposite.'

Radio conversation of correspondents in Kiev, Minsk, Kishinyov

Moscow Radio, 12 May 1986, 12–00

A phone-call like that was inevitable. At the other end of the line a woman's voice anxiously enquired: 'Where are your children? Oh, no answer eh? So a white Volga rolled up to your door and took your sons away to the Crimea. Meanwhile ours are here, squashed in...'

We would remind you once again, incidents of panic were vary rare. Calamity is being born with dignity.

Komsomolskaya Pravda, 7 May 1986

He was weeping his heart out. He was trying to suppress his tears, but it was no use. He let his head fall to the table, covered his face and feebly ran his toil-worn fingers, aged by labour, through his sparse greying hair. This old workman from Pripyat was grief-stricken. The fire at the Chernobyl nuclear station and the speedy evacuation, as he was, in his navy-blue track-suit and household slippers; he was taken tens of

151

kilometres to Ivankov. He thought he'd be away two or three days, he'd get by. He didn't. And on his hands for a long time had been his terminally ill old mother, enduring an agonizing death-bed.

Someone touched his shoulder, and said something comforting in a low tone...

(Anelia Perkovskaya, the Secretary of the Pripyat town council, helped dozens of frightened, confused people.)

Komsomolskaya Pravda, 11 May 1986

The evacuation from villages and hamlets was a trickier business. Not one peasant wanted to leave at the height of the spring season, many had not yet realized the degree of danger.

Moscow News, 1 June 1986

I have had to take part in suppressing outbreaks of cholera, be present at plague-spots, and visit leper-colonies. So therefore when I went out to the Ivankov and Poles'ye regions immediately adjacent to the thirty-kilometre zone, much of what I was to see in the hospitals and emergency stations seemed familiar from the beginning: the unusually large number of medical personnel, among whom were many visitors, yards crammed with ambulances, and health UAZs with number plates from every province in the Ukraine, offices for chief physicians, all looking like a military headquarters during the war.

But what was taking place there bore no resemblance whatever to events during the epidemics of the past: neither in the degree of rapidly escalating danger to the population nor in the scale of the numbers of people being moved.

Yuri Scherbak, Doctor of Medicine, writer
Literary Gazette, 21 May 1986

They also tell of those who taught children their first lesson in cruelty, of teachers who abandoned their children, betrayal indeed. It was a lesson in treachery which shocked the children.

We are all aware, particularly teachers, writers and doctors, that serious thought must now be given to softening the effects of the psychological trauma which the children have suffered. The problem exists and cannot be resolved merely by presents and amateur talent concerts in pioneer camps. One should read the letters of children from the south where conditions are excellent. The children mention the hospitality, the warmth of their welcome, but in these bright voices there are constant hints of disturbance and anxiety about their own homes.

Literary Gazette, 23 July 1986

CHAPTER 15

Anastasia penetrates the thirty-kilometre zone

They set off into the zone on bicycles. Shlik had rustled up a lady's bike for Anastasia, otherwise she couldn't have ridden, it being a form of transport totally forgotten since her childhood. They took with them rucksacks, bottled water and sandwiches together with pocket torches.

While they were pedalling through the village areas Anastasia coped somehow with her ancient boneshaker but once they reached the woods things got harder. The bicycle was forever swerving off the road and crashing into a tree. Still, it wasn't as hard as it became later ... Suddenly Shlik issued a muted command:

'Lights out, auntie. The zone.'

'But I can't see anything Shlik!'

The boy stopped, took out a white handkerchief and tied it on the back of his saddle.

'Keep your eyes on that white patch and get a grip on yourself. If you fall off, don't scream, they'll be on us like lightning. If they do pinch us, remember: you're responsible for the trip, I'm guiding you into the zone to look for your sister out of the goodness of my heart. Agreed?'

'Agreed,' confirmed Anastasia meekly.

At one especially hazardous spot they dismounted and pushed their machines. They passed a black board bearing the words 'Forbidden zone. Danger to life!' In the darkness, the words were clearly visible from a long way off. From then on the journey lay through woodland and scrub.

155

A couple of times they halted to have a drink; one of these stops was by a rivulet.

'Can we drink out of the stream at all?' asked Anastasia.

'That's out. It's everywhere about here, the radiation. And where there's more, or less, nobody knows. There are places at fifteen kilometres where the dosage is higher than in the station itself. There it is now, you can see it. See, the sky's glowing. That's the industrial compound. They're working night and day there. They're putting a cap on the reactor.'

'Why a "cap" exactly?'

'Because that's how they write about it in the papers – Chernobyl's not really a disaster for us, it's child's-play. They've forced people to work over there, soldiers. I pity the lads. I've been close and seen them working. There's not enough respirators even for them, so they're shovelling up that radiation wearing muslin masks, horrible.'

'Yet you go into the zone, aren't you afraid of radiation?'

'Who told you I wasn't? Only fools aren't afraid. I take iodine tablets and drink pure spirit every day. You see I want to pick up enough for one year of life, one year of living to my heart's delight, then they can put me in a hospital cot.'

He stopped talking, then went on quietly:

'I want to have me a time, auntie, once maybe twice more into the zone, then off to the south. What have the little soldiers got for being heroes? OK, they get some leave. In the morning the choppers fly in, their helicopters. So there's lead screening in every helicopter. I talked to one of the pilots. He laughed and said: "If you want to be a dad, sheathe your dick in lead, my lad." He's got to laugh about it, otherwise you might as well drown yourself. Still he flew up to the reactor and dropped his bags of sand and clay and then back to base. But the soldier in his muslin is in the zone day and night. So that's how it is, auntie! Now that's enough sitting about here for us. The most dangerous part's just ahead; we've got to nip across the main road. Come on!'

They mounted their cycles and set off once more. The moon rose and by its light Anastasia could see the white patch of Shlik's handkerchief. The going didn't get much easier though: the road lead through bushes and the branches whipped across her face unmercifully.

Soon the monotonous roar of traffic could be heard. Shlik slowed.

'We're going along through the bushes parallel to the road now, then we'll dash across.'

The roaring became ever more distinct and soon the wet road could be glimpsed between the bushes. Anastasia already knew that this road was sprinkled specially to wash away radioactive dust. It flashed across her mind that this water would run off the road afterwards and possibly reach the path they were now using, laying down a stratum of radiation.

Soon Shlik leaped from his cycle and signed to Anastasia to follow suit. They stood behind a wide-spreading shrub. Before them was a bend in the road stretching away in both directions on the far side of the dark wall of vegetation. Shlik seized her arm powerfully and said in a low voice:

'We have to wait now, till there's a hold-up on the road. Then we'll nip across.'

They had a long time to wait. Vehicles were moving in one direction virtually without pause, the direction where the sky glowed over the industrial site. Only one or two vehicles, mostly lightweight, came flashing back the other way. But gradually vehicles became fewer and at length the flow ceased. The road was deserted. Shlik pulled Anastasia by the sleeve and tore across the highway, head down, cycle held by the handlebars. Anastasia ran after him, banging her leg painfully on a pedal as she ran, and was not left behind.

There was no path on the other side of the highway and they went on pushing their way through the roadside undergrowth trying not to entangle their wheels in stray branches. At length a small protrusion appeared and Shlik went towards it.

'Pill-box. Left here since the war as a memorial. We'll rest up in there a bit and have a swig. From now on it's bikes; this path leads straight to the settlement.'

The rest was a short one and no torches were used: vehicles on the highway roared past a few yards away. They were soon on their way again. They hid their cycles in the bushes at the entrance to the settlement and went forward on foot. Shlik crept confidently along the fences, guiding Anastasia through back yards and the shrubs of children's playgrounds. At one spot he suddenly tore at her shoulder:

'Down! Cops!'

Not far away, a police car was nosing along the wide street.

'Patrol,' elucidated Shlik, when the car was hidden round the bend. 'They go all round here once a night. That was lucky, they won't be back. They don't want more X-rays than they have to either.'

They emerged on a broad street with tall blocks of flats. By the light of the moon, these monsters with their dead, black windows seemed menacing. Anastasia felt her heart thump, stabbing painfully, whether from excitement or the over-exertion of her nocturnal journey.

'Well, this is your Energy Prospect. Which house was it then?'

'Forty-two.'

'Over there in those blocks. Let's go!'

They approached one of the tall buildings. The numbers were clearly visible from afar. Shlik pulled at the handle of the entrance door and it opened obediently.

'Either they forgot to lock it or somebody's been here already. Come on then, I'll open the door of your flat, then have a scout round the next-door houses. Somebody's been in this one before me, obviously.'

They climbed up to the third floor. The door had the name-plate 'Prikhotko I'. What lay in wait for her? The answer or just another useless step? Shlik got a bunch of keys including skeleton-keys out of his pocket and examined the lock.

'French? A pushover. Look, the door's just been banged-to. In a hurry, obviously.'

The door opened soundlessly. In the depths of the flat a window glimmered, apparently wide-open.

Anastasia stood on the threshold and heard the thumping of her heart.

'Well, go on in, don't waste time. Close the curtains

158

straight away and then use the torch, got it? I'll have a rake round and come back for you. Bye for now, auntie!'

Shlik slid away down the staircase, a noiseless shadow.

Anastasia entered the flat. She stood for a moment letting her eyes get used to the almost total darkness, then went to the window, closed it and drew the curtains. She now felt able to switch on the torch, keeping it pointed downwards as Shlik had taught her. It was the sitting-room. Sofa, two armchairs, circular table, book-case. In the corner, a writing-desk. Neat and tidy everywhere as if the owners were asleep in the next room. Anastasia went over to the table and drew her hand across the surface. Even by the dim light of the torch she could see that her palm was covered with a thick layer of dust. Anastasia wiped her palm on the hem of her dress and walked into the next room. It was the bedroom and nursery combined. Opposite the large double bed stood two empty children's cots side by side and a toy cupboard next to them. The little beds were unmade and the blankets lay in untidy heaps. The double bed was disarranged on one side only.

Further on was a windowless bathroom. Anastasia automatically touched the light-switch and gasped and slammed the door shut behind her. The bathroom was flooded with light. She gazed round. Washing-machine, a pile of children's underthings on it. Here also everything was covered in dust, blown in through the open sitting-room door probably.

Anastasia extinguished the light and went out into the corridor again. Kitchen. Tidy everywhere, and powdered from above by the ubiquitous dust. How quickly it had flown in! Kettle on the stove. Refrigerator. For some reason Anastasia opened this a little but clapped it to at once; the light had gone on here as well. Dim, of course, but no sense in taking risks.

A cup stood on the table and Anastasia saw the remains of tea at the bottom. There was bread in the bin. It had turned into one huge rusk by now. Sugar. Pot of jam. Good God, between the sugar and jam Anastasia glimpsed a sheet of paper. She snatched it, blew the dust from it and brought the torch close up to it.

'Ivanushka! I got up to look at the children and saw the glow over the station. It must be a fire. I tried to phone through but it's always engaged. I'm going to run over to find out what's happened. The children are sleeping quietly, don't worry. If you get home before me, put the kettle on and wait for me. Alenka.'

Without fully taking in the sense of what she had read, Anastasia went into the bathroom with the note in her hand. There she closed the door tight and put the light on. She read the note through again closely. Then her head fell forward on to the pile of dusty children's underthings on the washing-machine and froze into immobility.

She came to as someone shook her by the shoulder. It was Shlik, back from his expedition.

'What's up, auntie? Did you fall asleep?'

Anastasia handed him the note. Shlik read it and whistled:

'Bloody hell! What made the fool run after her man? OK, nothing to be done now. Up you get, it'll be getting light soon.'

Anastasia tried to stand, but at once grabbed at the side of the machine.

'I can't walk, Shlik. Go back without me. I'll get out of here tomorrow somehow.'

'Tomorrow? Tomorrow the cops'll find you! Have you gone raving mad? You'll land me in it. Come on now, stand up! Let's go!'

Shlik was shouting at the top of his voice now, unafraid of being heard from the street.

'You can see Shlik, I can't budge. And there's the bike. No, you just leave me, Shlik, please.'

'You fool! You know how much radiation you'll pick up in a whole night? There won't be a hospital that'll accept you tomorrow.'

'Oh well, what difference does all that make now ... Go Shlik, go back. Don't hang about for my sake. If I'm alive you'll get your tape-recorder and jeans from abroad I promise.'

'Oh stuff your jeans up your arse. I don't bloody care.

How can I leave you here? There's rad-i-ation here! What an idiot, getting mixed up with you.'

Shlik was on the verge of hysteria. Collecting her last remaining reserves, Anastasia spoke to him in her teacher's voice.

'Now look here, young man. I'm not a little girl. I am responsible for myself. I shan't tell anyone a thing about you, you needn't worry about that. I'll get out of here. Now – be off with you. It really is dangerous for you to stay here.'

The classroom tone worked. Shlik relaxed, sighed and said:

'Well all right, I'll do as you say. Tomorrow do your best to get as far away from here as you can and go via the villages. Don't go near the highway. In the daytime the traffic's like the Kreschatik in Kiev. Keep well.'

Moving sideways, so as not to let out too much light into the corridor, Shlik left the bathroom and the sound of his footfalls died away.

Anastasia laid her head on the underthings once more. Through the odour of the dust there came a comical, childish smell Anastasia had long forgotten. Alenushka's little blouses and dresses had smelled like that once. Suddenly she recalled an old Russian fairy-tale she had read to her little sister. The one about sister Alenushka and brother Ivanushka. Ivanushka, turned into a goat by a wicked witch, stands on the bank and cries:

> Little sister Alenushka! Little sister Alenushka!
> Swim out, swim out on to the bank.
> The fire is hot and burning
> The kitchen spit is turning
> The wicked step-mother wants to kill me.

And his little sister answers from the bottom of the river:

> I cannot swim to you, brother Ivanushka!
> A white tomb-stone lies on my breast,
> Silken grasses entwine my feet,
> An evil snake sucks at my heart!

Anastasia sat on the floor, head buried in her arms, rocking from side to side, repeating over and over again the words of an old fairly-tale...

At length she forced herself to get up. She went over to the sink and turned on the tap. A thin stream of water emerged. Radioactive? She was indifferent. She rinsed her face and wet her blouse over the heart. It became slightly easier to breathe. She put out the bathroom light and went out into the kitchen. It was starting to lighten outside and she could do without the torch. She picked up the cup from which Alenushka had drunk for the last time and poured herself some water from the tap. She drank. She had forgotten the water from Ivankov still in the rucksack in the hallway. After that, she walked round the whole flat again, trying to commit it all to memory. In the bedroom, she went up to the children's cots. In one, a rabbit lay on the pillow, in the other a little bear was sitting on its hind legs. She took both toys and, hugging them to her, went out of Alenushka's home.

Outside it was almost daylight. In the distance the same unceasing din of work was audible but around her there was not a soul, not a whisper of movement. Anastasia walked through the dead town for a long time in the opposite direction to that of the noise. The stone houses came to an end, gardens and one-storey wooden cottages began. In the yard of one of these, Anastasia caught sight of some hens pecking in the dust. On the porch a sleek fox was sitting eyeing his foolish prey, staying conveniently close at hand. Occasionally one hen, even more stupid than the rest, came right up to the porch and the fox yelped quietly at her – demanding respect. Without showing the least anxiety, the hen would move off anyway. Did the hens take their destroyer for a domestic dog, put there to supervise them by their owners who had gone off somewhere? Anastasia conceived a vague hatred for this brazen predator and pity for the poor, thoughtlessly-submissive fowl. She was looking round for a stone to chase the insolent creature from the porch, when she heard above her head a subdued roaring, getting nearer. She instinctively concealed herself beneath the foliage of a nearby tree. It was

a helicopter flying over. 'They're capping the reactor ...'
She recalled Shlik's words. She went on down the street,
keeping close to the fence and trying not to linger in any
treeless space. She at once forgot about the fox and the
feeding hens.

The helicopters kept flying in one after another, but their
roaring soon ceased to impinge on Anastasia's conscious-
ness. She was walking with difficulty, forcing herself to
keep moving, where didn't matter. She felt that if she
stopped, her heart would immediately stop too. Movement
dulled the pain.

Anastasia was passing an inconspicuous little house, as
silent as all the others around it when she shuddered at a
quiet call:

'Daughter, little daughter! Wait on...'

She looked in the direction of the voice. There beyond
the fence, in the shade of a big lilac bush, stood a tiny old
woman with a stick. She was dressed in a long, dark skirt
and a grey knitted cardigan. She had a kerchief on her head,
white as sweet-peas, tied low over her eyes, so that no hair
could escape. The old woman beckoned to her. Anastasia
moved closer, bewildered and afraid of this figure, so
incongruous here in these unpeopled places. If an expert in
protective clothing had accosted her with a dosimeter, she
would have been less afraid.

'Who ... are you?' asked Anastasia, growing cold.

'I'm a local here, I live here. You haven't a bit of bread
have you, my girl?'

The old woman also came nearer the fence and put her
dry dark hand on the rickety wood. On the hand, Anastasia
made out patches, resembling bruises, but the old woman's
dark eyes peeping out from under her kerchief were lively
and welcoming. In her other hand she was holding a
number of eggs.

'So you don't have any bread then?' She repeated her
question. Only now did Anastasia realize that this was no
vision, but a real, live, woman.

'Granny! What on earth are you doing here? How did you
come to be here, all on your own?'

'I'm telling you aren't I? I live here. Living out my time.

163

Just you come in to my little garden. There's the gate there.'

Anastasia saw the wicket-gate some yards away and walked in.

'So you didn't go with the evacuation, Granny?'

'What?' asked the old woman, cupping her ear. 'The evacuation, you say? They went and forgot about me. No time for me, took my grandchildren. They'll live and I'm to die on my own. Still, it's better that way, so it is. If I die soon, best be at home, and in it I'll die. It's good they've forgotten me. There's other old folk sat it out down in the cellars, hid themselves from the evacuation.'

'So you're not on your own here?'

'There's others ...' she said slyly, as it seemed to Anastasia. 'And what about you, who might you be? Work here, or what?'

'No, I've come from a long way away. I was looking for my sister Alenushka here.'

'Find her?'

'No. She's missing, Granny.'

'Perished, you say,' said the deaf old woman. 'Well that's better than being ill. For the young ones it's terrible, I've seen. Us, the oldies, just burn out, quiet like, but what's it like for them who've not lived long in the world? Better if it happens all at once ... So your sister's with God. Those martyrs I expect God took to himself straight away. Innocent they were and it was a cruel death for them ... but let's go into the hut, why're we standing here to be seen? If anybody goes past, they'll see. They come round here sometimes ... come on girl. Oi, you're not young at all now I look at you. Your hair's all grey, like mine used to be. But I see you've got a short skirt, stepping out straight, well, I think – a girl. But you're getting on ...'

So saying, the old woman took Anastasia into the house. Across the verandah they passed into a spotless kitchen. It smelt of freshly scrubbed floors and lilac. A large bunch of it stood in a jug on a plain unadorned table. A kettle was boiling on the electric plate on a bench under the window. The old woman went up to it, lifted off the lid and lowered the eggs into the water.

'At first we used to eat them raw but the current came on again so we boil them on the stove. My little hens lay, there's onion in the garden, parsley, potatoes in the cellar and lard in the pantry. I get by. So you've got nothing either, you say? Never mind, we'll have breakfast without bread.'

While listening to the old woman, Anastasia was gazing about the kitchen. In the space between the windows, she noticed a mirror and walked over to it. Yes, her hair certainly was white, though it was filmed over with dust. Only yesterday there had been just a touch of grey at the temples ... Anastasia drew a hand across her face.

'I could do with a wash...'

'There's a washbasin in the corner yonder. Don't wash too hard though, I've got a tedious long way to go for water. I bring a bucket back at night to last me all day. How do you like eggs, hard-boiled or city-style?'

'Doesn't matter. Anyway I've got no appetite, Granny.'

'What's all this "granny" all the time? What do they call you?'

'Anastasia.'

'There, that's a really nice name. Anastasia. Well, and from your father?'

'Nikolayevna.'

'Nikolayevna, then. And I'm Lukyanishna. Sit up to table and we'll have breakfast.'

Anastasia, having rinsed her face and hands under the tap, wiped them on a hand-sewn towel hanging nearby and sat down on a bench. Lukyanishna placed an egg before her, then the salt-cellar and finally a white onion sprouting green shoots. Anastasia picked up the egg and started to roll it pensively about the table.

'Now don't play about with it. You're not little. Go on and eat it!'

'Lukyanishna, don't you want to go away from here? Where the people are?'

'And why should I leave? My neighbour Makarovna, lives three streets away, was evacuated with hers at first, and came back on the third day. Just couldn't stand it, that evacuation. Among strangers, and they were scared of ours,

165

bringing a plague to them. One of her grandsons got sick, so they took him and the rest from the mother and carted him off somewhere. No clothes, no bed-clothes, they put them all on the floor. Makarovna felt terrible, looking at all that mess, so back she came on the quiet.'

'Are there a lot like that?'

'Oh no, not many now, they're dying off. But at least it's at home in their own bed. No comparison there, strange folk. Here there's some point in washing up and Gaffer Yegor reads prayers out of the book. He can't get up, he's paralysed. But his book's very old, important, came from the forefathers. It's written there about Chernobyl as well.'

'What's written about Chernobyl? How can that be if the book's very old?'

'Well now, only the ancient books have the truth written in them, dear. It says there that at the end of the world, there will be all kinds of warnings to folk. And one warning says this: an Angel will light a star over the earth called Wormwood, and wormwood in our talk is Chernobyl. It's not just chance, is it? And fire will fall from that star Wormwood on the sources of rivers and they will be poisoned. Well now, isn't that so? You and I'll go up the ladder into the attic and you'll see what they're doing in the town: washing the houses, stripping off the earth as if from a dead cow. They're washing the dust off the houses, but the poisoned water's soaking into the earth again, to make streams under the earth, spreading all over and poisoning the whole district. Scurrying about like ants, but the wrath of God cannot be washed away with water, no! We're off to one side but you can see it all in the distance. Those doing the washing are picked up and carted away as well. Ambulances and doctors always going, always going ... And Gaffer Yegor also says that this warning is not the last. The star Chernobyl will burn out and folk will have a breathing-space, so they can think. And if they don't, then a terrible pestilence will come down upon them. But you can hear Gaffer Yegor yourself. I'll take you there through the gardens after breakfast. He lies there, poor thing, on his own till evening, then when it gets dark we all get together at his place. Anybody missing, we go to their place. A burial, that means. So you'll go with me? Gaffer's got to be turned over, and washed. Otherwise he smells too bad, diarrhoea with blood comes out of him. Soon it'll be over. So you can help me.'

'I'll go with you, Lukyanishna. And tonight I'll bring some bread and things,' said Anastasia, recalling that the rucksack was still in the hall of Alena's flat.

'My, my! And we haven't had any bread for ever so long ... But why aren't you eating anything? Still grieving for your sister? Whose toys are those you've got?'

'My nephews'.'

'And where are they?'

'Don't know, Lukyanishna. Everything points to their evacuation. Maybe the neighbours took them. They'll have to be looked for now.'

'Ah, that means you'll be going away, does it?' said Lukyanishna, disappointed, or so it seemed to Anastasia. 'And here was I thinking you'd be stopping with us, at the grave of your sister like.'

'I can't, Lukyanishna, I'll stay for a while then I'll go back there to the people, and look for my nephews. I have to give them to somebody to bring up now.'

'Haven't you got any other family?'

'There's another sister, the middle one, but she's further away than Alenushka. She lives abroad, has done for ages.'

'Well she'll come back, when she hears the trouble that's happened, kiddies on their own. Did she love her sister, the one that's at rest?'

The phrase struck Anastasia's heart with renewed force. She fought against giddiness and rubbed her eyes.

'You yourself now, not ill are you?' Nikolaina Lukyan-ishna suddenly asked, looking at her. 'Radiation?'

'I've got a bad heart. I don't know about radiation. On the way here we went through dangerous places and I've got covered in dust since. But don't worry, I'll stay with you and help you. I can get water and food for you at least. How could I abandon you, old and sick as well?'

'How on earth can you carry water with a bad heart?'

'Well, who else is going to do it? Soon as it's dark I'll go for it.'

'See what a heart it is you've got; it aches with sickness and grief but it sees people. To grieve too much is a sin. There, your eyes are dry as dry and you just keep looking at the wall. You should cry a bit, I expect you haven't cried yet? At all?'

Anastasia shook her head.

'There you are then, that's it. Tears are given to us to wash out grief from the heart, otherwise it grows so scabbed, that heart, that after that nobody or their misfortune can find a way in. Have a little cry, have a little cry, I tell you. Just put your arms on the table, head on top, come on. Cry, I tell you!'

Lukyanishna laid out Anastasia's arms and with her black-spotted dry hand pressed her head towards the table. Anastasia obediently lowered her head and began to weep and cry out loudly. Lukyanishna embraced her and she, too, began to cry.

On Saturday 26 April at three o'clock in the morning I was awoken by the phone ringing and went quickly to the assembly field. We arrived in Kiev by plane and later Chernobyl. The information was alarming. In Moscow we had heard that the accident was not a straightforward one but what we saw demonstrated how grim the situation actually was.

Yevgeni Ignatenko,
deputy head of 'Soyuzatomenergo'
Radio Mayak, 24 May 1986, 11–00

There's an expression current here: 'how much did you get?' So the deputy head of Soyuzatomenergo, Ignatenko, 'got' a lot, several tens of rontgens. But he's an expert and knows the permitted levels. 'Nothing terrible,' he says confidently. 'There's some with more.'

Soviet Russia, 13 May 1986

Five rontgens per year is the norm for a worker at a nuclear power-station. If he gets more than twenty-five in a year he is taken off the job.

Academician Leonid Ilyin
Pravda Ukraine, 16 May 1986

On 27 April the highly experienced pilots B. Nesterov and A. Serebryakov flew in with the first crews. They drew up a schedule of approach to the reactor where sacks could be dropped. The first sacks were filled with sand by everybody at once. How were they dropped? They hovered over the crater, opened the door and, aiming at the hole by eye, let go. And it wasn't rays of sunlight coming up out of that accident block. And everybody knew that very well, but their first thought was the sacks. There weren't many and they were soon exhausted. The general roared off in his UAZ to the nearest village and collected loads more from the yards.

Red Star, 7 June 1986

Ten days after the accident, the danger of it spreading still existed.

Pravda, 13 May 1986

On the road to the nuclear power-station at Chernobyl, to left and right, there are hundreds of vehicles, construction equipment. The army is rendering enormous service in coping with the accident.

Trud, 21 May 1986

A serious problem is the burial of radioactive debris, surface layers of earth removed by the bulldozers, tree-trunks irradiated in the fallout zone of the explosion, water used to cool the damaged reactor, now drained off into special tanks. Anything which constitutes a hazard must be securely isolated. The construction of these so-called 'burial grounds', however, demands considerable resources, technical equipment and, most important, time.

Izvestiya, 24 July 1986

We are isolating block four and then, in order, comes the restoring of the first three blocks to life; they can and must work. We are also considering when construction work on blocks five and six should resume.

Komsomolskaya Pravda, 13 May 1986

All the area from Chernobyl to Kiev can't be sprinkled but every yard of the roads is washed most carefully.

Socialist Industry, 10 June 1986

Every three hours the miners relieve each other at the power-station underground, coolly and courageously carrying out their appointed task.

Moscow Radio, 19 May 1986, 19–00

Among the vehicles you can encounter here on the Chernobyl streets, ambulances are numerous.

Radio Mayak, 23 May 1986

Soldiers, NCOs and officers are working with
exceptional selflessness and, on occasions, heroism.
As circumstances require, the military detachments
relieve one another here – an understandable concern
for people's health of course.

Moscow Radio, 19 May 1986

In only two days, 19 and 20 May, more than 1,000
donors in Gomel Province have given blood.

Moscow Radio, 6 June 1986, 12–00

Pripyat looks odd and unusual seen from a helicopter.
Snow-white, multi-storey buildings, wide avenues,
parks and stadiums, games courts alongside
kindergartens and shops ... The town is empty. Not a
single person on the streets and in the evening not a
lighted window.

Pravda, 6 May 1986

The malicious tongues only say that people who like
living on other people's goods go wandering round the
empty towns and villages.

Police colonel Dmitri Chaus
Soviet Russia, 10 June 1986

All the same, there have been cases where people
have tried to get back into their own house. It's
understandable: they've left belongings there, even the
flowers need watering...

Moscow Radio, 26 May 1986

They went round the flats checking that everybody had
gone. It turned out not all had.

Komsomolskaya Pravda, 11 May 1986

The young couple had not only fled from the town in
panic, but left an invalid father in the flat. The police
evacuated the father, after seeing a light burning in the
window when the town was already empty.

Pravda, 23 May 1986

171

Two old women were sent into hospital at the end of
May: Anastasia Stepanova Semenyak, born 1901,
living on Stalingrad Heroes Street, 10, flat 114 and
Maria Ivanovna Karpenok, born 1912, living on
Kurchatov Street, 27, flat 8. During the mass
evacuation, they hid themselves so well no one could
find them. It was only on 28 and 29 May that they came
out of their retreats.

Soviet Russia, 10 June 1986

CHAPTER 16

Anna and Sven take a decision

The weather couldn't make up its mind. In general it was quite warm but a sudden wind would rush into the valley and blanket the mountains in cloud; soon a thunderstorm was in full swing. Occasionally the downpour caught Anna and Sven out walking and every time they came back to the house soaked to the skin, the landlady would remind them:

'You must take a shower! The rain is very dangerous now – radiation.'

At length Sven could contain himself no longer and whispered to the landlady not to keep reminding Anna about radiation: 'Anna had a sister in Chernobyl...' From that day on the landlady was especially attentive to Anna.

On days of lowering weather they occupied themselves with work. Back in Stockholm, Sven had been seized with the idea of publishing an anthology of unofficial Russian women poets. He had already translated almost all there was of Irina Ratushinskaya and the Leningrad women, whom Anna knew personally. In Heidelberg she had several folders of their poems and regretted that she couldn't show them to Sven at once. Still, she knew a good many by heart and read him one after the other, everything she could recall.

On one occasion she read him Yelena Ignatova's poem about Lot's wife:

You will turn back then...'No!'
You will turn back then...'No!'
...and in your city see
That yellow smoking glow.

'The streams, what have they said?'
...There's ashes there and dust.
Above the angel's head
Two blazing pinions thrust.

'They were all sinners.' Yes.
'They were all guilty.' Yes.
Sin's nakedness must bear
The brand of fire's impress.

'I will not turn. I'll hold
And make the tempter flee.
By river banks of gold
The Lord God leadeth me.'

By river banks of gold
The Lord God leadeth thee?
Their cries then find you cold,
The charred flesh leaves you free?

The child that's running there –
The burning star's caress...
You weep? 'I cannot bear...
The body turns and – Yes!'

Having read through to the end in a faltering voice Anna
fell silent. She went over to Sven, who was sitting at the
table, knelt down in front of him and hid her head between
his knees. He stroked her trembling shoulders in silence.

She lifted her wet face to him:

'Sven, I absolutely do not know what to do now.'

'What can we do now, Annie? We have to wait. Not long
now. Anastasia will find out about Alenka. She found Ivan
– dead, but she found him. God will help her to find his
children alive.'

174

'It's the fourth day and no phone-call.'

'Maybe they just won't let her phone us. The Kiev KGB could sniff out when she's ringing you. We know they don't want the truth about Chernobyl to get out to the West.'

'True enough...Remember Sven, I kept telling you I couldn't explain the differences between freedom and liberty. But it looks as if I can now. At the moment I'm free as never before, but I have no liberty of action. I am not at liberty to help my sisters in any way, my helplessness is crushing me. Whereas our Anastasia who restricted her whole life on our account and her party's, she's doing everything possible and impossible, she's breaking through every barrier and taking it all on her own shoulders, all of it! She has the liberty. I've got freedom, and how! I even have happiness – you. But I've lost the possibility of exercising my will. If I was at home, no Soviet authority, no Gee Bees could stop me finding Alenushka alive or dead.'

'Patience, Annie, have patience! You're at the standstill point at the moment, there's nothing you can find out and nobody you can help; but that's just for the time being. Once Anastasia rings we'll find something out at least and then we can decide what to do. Your sisters are going to need money. We'll leave ourselves just enough to start life together, and my hunting-lodge. I haven't got the strength to part with that. The rest we can send to your sisters. Alenushka,' he faltered for a second, 'probably lost everything, like everybody from Chernobyl. That way we can help them start a new life, right Annie?'

Anna nodded, by now somewhat reassured.

'Right. After that we'll get married and decide where best to live – Germany or Sweden. We'll fix up living-quarters and get down to work, not just our own, I mean joint translations. We'll publish a book of your women friends and then one of Irina Ratushinskaya. There was something else I wanted to say...' Sven broke off suddenly and then added equally unexpectedly, 'Just sit properly, I can't see your face.' Anna seated herself at the table and prepared to listen.

'I have to admit, Annie, that in the first days I thought you had an unjustifiably tragic attitude. The West took it all

175

as a terrible accident, a sensation even, but no one took it as a tragedy close to their hearts. A bit like our landlady here grieved over her losses like the other peasants in Germany, Italy and Austria. It took me these two weeks being next to you to see that what had happened was a crushing blow for everyone. Chernobyl is a warning. So far, your propaganda is right but it focuses attention on nuclear tests in the USA and so gains the advantage. But there's more at stake than that. See how much attention is placed on nuclear accidents in the West in the Soviet press. If even a tenth was true all nuclear stations would have to close tomorrow. Of course they're using the facts to reassure the Soviet reader I realize...'

'Yes, but the opposite effect is achieved!' Anna broke in. 'The Soviet reader, hearing about all these accidents in the West, starts to think: If they have all this trouble with their technology, what's going to happen in our own stations with the well-known "tufta" we have to put up with?'

'What's "tufta" Anna?'

'Ah, sorry. It's a camp word. It means putting on a show of work to impress the boss, to get your bread ration.'

Sven nodded, he knew what that was. Anna continued:

'In general I agree with you, Sven. Humanity isn't mature enough for the atom. And in Soviet hands it's like giving a madman a box of matches, what with their paranoid urge to astonish the world and their mania for doing things on the cheap: sooner or later there's going to be a fire. I just can't be detached enough about Chernobyl yet to see the essential meaning of it as a tragedy. It's my own I keep thinking about.

'Sometime you and I'll be able to talk about all this and think in a more balanced way...'

It was getting brighter outside, the rain had ceased and Sven proposed a walk by the river.

They were walking along the road looking at the rise in the river after the cloudburst. Anna suddenly caught sight of some dense clumps of green down by the water.

'Sven, I think that's mint. Let's pick some and brew up some mint tea.'

She broke off a number of stems.

176

'Yes, marvellous smell, mm! But I don't think we should use them for tea. You know...'

Anna sighed.

'Heavens, you can't forget it for a second, there's no let-up. You know, when we lived in Svir, Alenushka was the one who dealt with the plants and herbs. She found herself a friend, a country wife, and she taught her the different plants. Anastasia and I hadn't a clue. If you'd only known what a girl she was, our Alenushka.'

'Why was, Annie? No need for that.'

'"Was", because I'm talking about years long past. Lord, how long ago all that was! The village, Nastya's school and us, two little idiots. Of course I thought I was oh, so clever. I read a lot and I was always trying to be top of the class. Alenushka didn't care what marks she got or what the teachers or her classmates thought. She learned only what interested her and skimmed through the rest, quite happy to get average marks. But if Nastenka wasn't pleased with her, she used to tear into her books and improve all her marks by the end of term; she only did it to please her sister. Everything she did, everything in the world, was so that somebody else should be happy. Even when she was little – for example, we'd be carrying water to the garden, she'd ask: "We're bringing the water, who's going to be pleased? Nastenka, isn't she? And the cabbages, aren't they?" When Nastya and I were arguing who she would stay with, the silly thing, she probably thought we both wanted to be rid of her, Nastya didn't want her again and I didn't want to haul her off into emigration. But she did find her Ivan. Before the wedding she told us as much: "I have to have at least one person who thinks of me as a joy, not a burden." I don't know about Nastya, but I couldn't talk her round. I just burn inside thinking about it. Oh, if only they find her!'

And she went on telling Sven about what Alenushka had been like as a child and how she had been loved by all who knew her.

'All the dogs in the street just came up to her. Saw her coming and smiled the way dogs do, can you imagine? And she talked to flowers. Yes, flowers, it does happen! She

177

sometimes stands in front of a tomato plant and gives it a telling off: "Where d'you think you're growing to? I'm asking you? What are you, a poplar or something? It's time you flowered, stop climbing up and up. You're a naughty plant. So tomorrow, come on, flowering time." And what do you think? Nastya and I laugh: "Well, and have you talked your tomato round?" and she answers so seriously: "Yes, I've talked the lazy thing round. Come and have a look, the first cluster is out."'

As she spoke of Alena, Anna seemed to thaw, glow even, and Sven was happy to listen to the end.

As soon as they walked into the house the landlady called to Anna:

'A call from Kiev for you!'

Anna ran downstairs and was away fifteen minutes. When she came back into the room, her face looked awful.

'Sven! Something terrible's happened. Anastasia's gone into the zone and not come back. Her Kievan friend says her heart had been very bad the previous few days. Now he's searching for her and stirred everybody up. He swears he'll find her and fetch her out of the zone.'

Sven hugged her in silence.

'That's not the end of it. Alenushka's children have been found. They've turned up in the Odessa children's hospital for some reason. Both boys are sick. Now let me go. I'm going to lie down. I feel unwell myself.'

Anna lay for several hours, her eyes closed, but Sven could see that she wasn't asleep. On occasion she would even open her eyes and glance at him, as if bringing to mind where she was and who was with her, before closing them once more. Towards evening she got up and asked for hot coffee. When Sven came up to the room bringing a tray with coffee and sandwiches, Anna was already on her feet. Her suitcase stood in the middle of the room and she was packing.

'Annie?' Sven's voice held a question.

'Yes, Sven. I've got to get back to Heidelberg.'

'Why now all of a sudden? It can wait till tomorrow. It's started raining again, that'll make the mountain roads tricky; it'll give you a bit of time to recover as well.'

'Sven! I'm going on the train by myself. You and I have got to separate.'

She tried not to look at Sven, hiding her face as she had done on the day of their first intimacy. But it was different then; Sven had realized how Anna was feeling. Now he saw her back bowed under a terrible weight, and that stubborn chin. Her voice sounded muffled and indifferent.

'Annie, get a grip on yourself! You can leave your packing for a minute or two and explain your decision. I have a right to know.'

'Better not. I've decided and that's enough. Forgive me and don't try to stop me.'

'I can't stop you, you're free to do as you like, but it's not just your future you're deciding now, it's mine too. So answer me, what's happened to make me of no account any more?'

'I've decided to go back to the Soviet Union. I've got to return there.'

'But that's impossible! They'd never let you back!'

Anna turned to face him and Sven saw that she was smiling with lips tensed. After a moment's silence, she spoke:

'There are plenty of ways of going back without asking anybody's gracious permission, Sven. I'll use one of them. No one's going to stop me whichever road I go. And I'm going, I've made up my mind.'

'So, I see...That's your will, your liberty. You want to exchange freedom for liberty?'

'No, Sven, I don't want anything for myself except to be a person. The children are ill and their parents...I can't allow Anastasia, sick as she is, if she's alive at all, to take it all on her shoulders again. It's not right that a person has to be a hero over and over again throughout her life, while others look after their own affairs or make their name in public affairs, literature and so forth. Damn all that, forget it. There's only one important thing for me now – find those children and replace their mother, like Anastasia did once for me and Alenushka. Incidentally, she also gave up her fiancé for our sake. You realize I can't land you with my future, if there's nothing to look forward to at all. You

179

aren't responsible for any of it, why take on someone else's woes?'

Sven sighed and sat down opposite Anna.

'Well, I realize this is a family thing for you: taking everything on yourself, leaving nothing for anyone else. Thanks for being so concerned over my peace of mind. And now don't interrupt, Annie. You've said the main thing already and you're starting to talk rubbish. Let's have some coffee and keep quiet for a while. I have to do some thinking and my blasted head's splitting. We walked too long in the rain.'

Anna stared steadily at him.

'You think it's something serious – your headache I mean?'

'Well of course, what could be more serious than my head-cold?' Sven smiled wryly. 'Pour me some of that coffee and keep quiet please.'

Anna shrugged and poured out coffee for them both. They drank in silence, then Sven spoke:

'Annie, I've started thinking with my aching head and something stirs, some preliminary ideas. Like this, it's best if you don't go back to the Soviet Union, but your husband goes instead, a Swedish citizen. I'll go to Kiev, find Anastasia's friends and put myself in the picture. Then I'll go on to Odessa, locate the children and demand that the Soviet authorities release them to me as my nephews. If they refuse, I'll keep on demanding. We'll raise a campaign for our kiddies. That's what we'll do, Annie, and we'll scrabble them out like Carlsson did with his Faina. So that's it, Annie. You have to agree, you haven't got the stupidest husband in the world. Well?'

Anna walked up to Sven and put her arms round him. 'Forgive me...'

'I'll forgive you, but promise there'll be no more of this in the future. The next time you feel like taking another important and wise decision consult me first.'

Anna nodded.

'Well now, that's fine. And now I have to go to bed, otherwise tomorrow my cold will be too bad for us to set off.'

'And what am I going to do?' asked Anna, smiling through her tears.

'You keep the flies away, like an exemplary biblical wife – and don't turn into a pillar of salt. That might be beautiful but highly inappropriate while we can still move and get something done.'

In the ensuing silence they heard a thrush whistle in the garden, drying after the rain, and the landlady rattling the pail as she prepared to go and fill it with milk that no one would drink.

Telebridge   Leningrad–Boston   Central   Television
17 June 1986, 19–35

American girl: I would like to know about Chernobyl. When you heard about the accident, what was your reaction?

Russian girl: You know... Of course, we heard about it only some time later. And of course, the first feeling was alarm. Alarm and fear...

Second Russian girl: (intervening decisively) Not fear! We just wanted to help, help and help again. We all wanted just one thing, that *you* should think about what would happen if... Anyway, I'm sorry, I get very emotional. We went through the same thing with Challenger. Challenger and Chernobyl are a warning to us. Girls, let's all fight as hard as we can for peace!

Third Russian girl: We can't get away from it. We can't close these stations. And you can't close yours. Nobody can. We must try to see that your scientists and ours get together and work to make them as safe as possible.

American girl: Seven years ago when we had the accident at Three Mile Island, it was on a much smaller scale than the Chernobyl accident. But as a result of it, the shares in atomic industries fell. Now there's a move in our country towards alternative forms of energy, which of them should be promoted. These alternative energy sources do exist after all. Our people were angry. What do you think of this?

SILENCE